POWER LINES

POWER LINES
What to Say
in 87 Problem Situations

Dr. Lynn Weiss
and
Lora Cain

Taylor Publishing Company
Dallas, Texas

Published by Taylor Publishing Company
1550 West Mockingbird Lane
Dallas, Texas 75235

Designed by Deborah Jackson-Jones

Library of Congress Cataloging-in-Publication Data

Weiss, Lynn.
 Power lines : what to say in problem situations / Lynn
Weiss and Lora Cain.
  p.   cm.
 ISBN 0-87833-736-9 : $14.95
 1. Interpersonal communication. 2. Self-
disclosure. 3. Assertiveness training. I. Cain, Lora.
II. Title.
BF637.C45W378   1991
158'.2—dc20   91-7903
                                                CIP

Printed in the United States of America

10 9 8 7 6 5 4 3 2 1

TABLE OF CONTENTS

ACKNOWLEDGMENTS

Many thanks for being allowed to experience and express my part of the information in this book.

My assistance has come from many sources:

Lora Cain, my co-author and friend;

My mentors, Tunaca and Altrondra;

The many people who have shared their life experiences with me;

My editor, Mary Kelly, who's taught me a lot about thinking in an orderly manner while at the same time sensitively supporting me throughout;

My friends and staff members who have helped with all the loose ends;

And my sons, Aaron and Mendel who have tolerantly hung in there while I've been learning and growing.

L.W.

I could never have completed this without the many people who have believed in and helped me. Some special thanks go to:

My family and especially my grandfather for their guidance, for teaching me to love words, and for giving me all of these problem situations to figure out!

A.W., for his love and for showing me how well these words can work.

Mary Kelly, super editor and visionary.

Two very special teachers, Virginia Tyler and Elizabeth Repulski—one believed I could act and the other believed I could do anything, especially write.

To Diana Cain Rasper, Lynne Haze, and Donna Peddy, who pulled me through so many dark nights.

And especially to Lynn Weiss, who was my hero long before I met her.

L.C.

Special thanks to Trudy Coleman for staying up to all hours to help us.

L.W. and L.C.

INTRODUCTION

"Please take me out to dinner" is what you say in order to *ask for what you want.* It's a *Power Line.* It states clearly and directly what you need to say in a situation so that you have a chance of getting your needs met. If instead, you say, "Wouldn't you like to go out for dinner?" or "I'm too tired to cook," you've lowered the odds of getting what you want because you sound as if you're only making a suggestion or a complaint. With a simple, direct line, however, you've gained the power to get your needs met.

Knowing what to say or do in problem situations is an essential element in living a happy life. We figured that out only after stumbling through many experiences and ending up mad at ourselves, upset with other people, and still not any closer to getting what we needed. And then we realized that the power to get what we need is *already within us.* We wrote this book to remind you that you've got the power, too.

Power Lines are what we use to remind ourselves that we can get our needs met. They are simple statements that communicate solutions to the everyday problems of living; the kinds of problems we all face at one time or another. The situations we discuss are real ones that we've either confronted ourselves or discussed on our radio talk show, and they run the gamut from "How do I let go of the past?" to "How do I talk calmly to my kids?"

You may find all of this to be very familiar. You may already know what you need to do or say in a given situation. But you may also forget it all the very next time you need to use that knowledge. It can take a lot of training to maintain the right Power Lines so that they stick in your memory and influence your actions. If you find in this book a helpful Power Line, then use it as a cue: Write it down and stick the reminder on your mirror or refrigerator where you'll see it often. It will help trigger that Power Line in your mind when you're faced with an appropriate situation. And instead of being stuck or making the same mistake again, you'll know what to do and say to move through the problem and to triumph over it!

If you feel we are writing about your life when you read this book, then we've done our job. You're not alone in dealing with these situations. You're not alone in failing to get what you want out of them. We didn't write this book because it's what we know; it's what we live. Power Lines can help you succeed by reminding you what to say and do to meet your needs, and perhaps they'll help you avoid some of the problems altogether.

So read the explanations carefully, nod your head and laugh at how familiar the situations are, and put to good use the Power Lines. May they work the wonders for you that they have for us.

Lynn Weiss and Lora Cain

POWER LINES

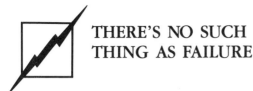

THERE'S NO SUCH THING AS FAILURE

You may have been told that failure is inescapable, but what you're really experiencing are only delays and detours. It is the way you look at a situation that counts. If you demand that you accomplish a certain project in a certain way within a certain time and one or all of the parameters are unmet, you will feel as if you have failed. But if you have a goal and you *keep* the goal *until* you achieve it, you will come to realize that you can succeed in anything you want by persisting.

Each delay can become a learning experience. Mistakes, too, provide us with opportunities to rethink, refine, and expand our goals. These detours can't be considered failures.

In school, passing and failing marks are only arbitrary cut-off points that mark someone else's idea of how learning is taking place and what constitutes success. In reality it is impossible to clearly divide success from failure. It is not a point in time or space, but rather a continuum of learning and refining one's awareness. Neither is it possible to define what success is. Wisdom comes as much from our errors as from our achievements. And success is whatever you think it is.

Rerouting your activities is not failure. If you discover that a particular course of action is not yielding the desired effect, you may choose a different course to reach your goal, or even a different path to follow. If the particular way you have designed to reach your goal is not working after considerable effort, you may want to reconsider the path or even the goal. An exchange of goals is only that: an exchange of goals. Quitting can be a powerful decision. You will have made a choice which carries power with it. When you feel powerful you'll feel in charge of your life.

YOU'VE GOT THE POWER

Whenever you are in a situation that makes you feel like a failure, your first job is to take care of your feelings. Nurture yourself and let your friends nurture you for a couple of days. There is nothing wrong with taking to your bed, but only for a day. Then get up and . . .

☐ Assess the situation.

☐ Analyze what really happened. Watch out about spending your time blaming others. That's a waste of your good time. Instead concentrate on yourself so you can gain the benefits of your analysis.

☐ Reassess your goals. What do you really want?

☐ Generalize your goal. Rather than saying, "I want to be manager of XYZ Company, say, "I want to be a manager." This gives you more chances of achieving your goal.

☐ Decide what you need to learn or to modify in yourself in order to reach your goal. This may be a practical skill or something emotional, such as developing trust in yourself.

☐ Decide whether you can reach your goal from your current position or if you need to make some kind of change.

☐ Ask for outside help to beat self-destructive patterns that are repeating in your life, so that you don't continue to make the same mistakes over and over.

☐ Be flexible, take a deep breath, and continue to pursue your goal.

WHAT TO DO AND SAY

▶ *You want to have a closer relationship with someone you especially like. However, that person tells you that she or he is not interested in a close relationship at this time, and then doesn't return your calls.*

When a personal relationship doesn't work out, realize it may have a lot more to do with the other person's needs rather than with your personal qualities. You will find someone who fits you better. Say to yourself, "It's the other person's loss. I'm lovable. I'll have an even better relationship in time."

▶ *You are not promoted to manager from the assistant position you have held for three years. Instead, someone who has worked there for a shorter period of time is made manager. You feel like a failure.*

If you were skipped over on the job, tell yourself, "I can stay here and make up for deficits I have. Or

I can go to another setting where I'll be appreciated more. If I keep my eyes open, my opportunities will come. I'm valuable regardless of my job."

▶   *You flunk an exam.*

If you flunk an exam, realize that it has little or nothing to do with your basic intelligence. It certainly doesn't mean you are intrinsically inadequate. It only means that in that area of study, at that time, you were unable to achieve. If your study habits are poor, say, "I can continue to pursue my goal and achieve it with hard work," and seek help to improve the way you study. If you find that you have no feeling for or real interest in *what* you are studying, then acknowledge this and say, "I can shift my goal to another area that fits me better." Once you correct the essential problem, tell yourself, "I will succeed."

NOW IS ALL YOU'VE GOT

Each of us experiences the passage of time differently at different times, depending upon how we feel and what we are doing. But the focus of attention is either in the present, the past, or the future. The quality of our lives depends a lot on where we place our focus: Ease of living and quality of life require us to focus in the present because there we have the least pain and the most power.

If you live in the past, you miss what's going on now. If you focus on the pain from an earlier bad situation, you continue to feel it over and over and over. The result is that you experience many times more pain than you did initially. Being unable to change the past, you are subject to feeling helpless. The sense of helplessness creates a secondary problem that is likely to affect your health and well-being.

On the other hand, if you focus too much on a past you remember as great, you are likely to live in a fantasy world, missing out on what's going on here. It will pull you away from the opportunity to have good experiences now. Reality can be pretty nice if you truly live with your eyes and heart open in the present time.

If you live in the future, you may characteristically worry about what might happen. Since you can't control the future, you will feel helpless much of the time. You will put off living, enjoying, and doing whatever you might want, because you'll always be planning for "someday."

If you always picture the future as rosy, you'll tend to be disappointed with the reality of it when it comes to pass. You'll also fail to live completely in the reality of the present and miss out on the stuff of life.

YOU'VE GOT THE POWER

Stop your activities several times a day and examine your thoughts. Ask yourself:

☐   "Am I aware of what I am doing?"

- ☐ "Am I taking on future problems before they even exist?"

- ☐ "Am I focusing on unfinished business from the past?"

- ☐ "Am I enjoying this moment?"

Use these questions to pull yourself back into the present.

WHAT TO DO AND SAY

▶ *A friend tells you that someone was interested in you, but you didn't notice. Instead, you were fantasizing about an ideal partner.*

Have a good talk with yourself, saying, "Pay attention. Open your eyes. Enjoy what is around you— NOW!" Have a friend help you focus by pointing out who and what is around you. Talk about what you both are seeing and compare observations. You'll sharpen your skills.

▶ *You sacrifice family fun and a social life to work day and night to get a promotion.*

Get your business and professional priorities in order. Tell yourself, "My family is important, and I choose to enjoy them now."

Then tell your boss, "I'm rearranging my professional and personal life so that I give quality time to both. This way, you'll have a top-class executive and my family will have a happier spouse and parent."

▶ *You don't have a personal life because you're waiting for a person you broke up with to come back.*

Let go of what is no more. Say, "I can let go of the past and will find someone new to love. That old love keeps me from enjoying people I meet now. I choose to let go of that person and enjoy now. I open my eyes to the present."

CHANGE IS THE ONLY SURE THING

No matter how much we resist, fight, or beg, we will find ourselves surrounded by change in our lives. During good times, change seems to come too quickly. During the bad times, it seems as if things will *never* change. Though we cannot regulate when the changes come in our lives, one thing is for certain: Nothing stays the same.

When we are caught up in our emotions, it seems as if we will always feel the way we're currently feeling. Remember how you felt when you have found yourself waiting—for anything—the letter in the mail, to hear about a job, to get out of the service, to be done with being pregnant. Remember the times when you were so happy you didn't ever want things to change. But, in time, changes in our feelings and life circumstances *do* occur.

YOU'VE GOT THE POWER

In *tough times,* remember you always have choices. You may not wish to pay the price of changing your situation, but you *can* change it if you want to badly enough. Whether you choose to stay in your current situation or not, you *do* have the power to change it.

☐ When you are in a situation that has you feeling blocked, trapped, or immobile, immerse yourself deeply in your feelings for five minutes. Then get up, breathe deeply, and do *something,* anything . . . even color in a coloring book or take a walk. Just start to move your muscles.

☐ Tell yourself that you *will* have a new job, a new love, or a new life.

☐ If you're struggling, tell other people, "I'm doing okay. I'm just dealing with my feelings." Then let others know what would be helpful, if anything.

In *good times,* it is important to enjoy what you have when you have it.

When things are going well for you, it is not unusual to meet someone who can't stand it. That person is likely to threaten you with a look of "Oh, sure, but don't expect it to last too long," which means, "Just wait, you'll get yours." If this happens, smile at this intrusive bearer of bad news and say, "So, be happy for me. I understand the ups and downs of life, but I intend to enjoy my good times fully."

If the person is especially offensive, you might add, "I'm sorry that you cannot enjoy my happiness with me. That would be a great gift for both of us."

WHAT TO DO AND SAY

▶ *You fell deeply in love during summer vacation with someone who lives in another city. Back in the daily routine, you are anxiously waiting to hear from the person.*

As you wait to hear from your summer love, say to yourself, "If it is meant to be, we will stay connected. I am lovable and capable of loving. If it's not that person, it will be another."

▶ *You are being evaluated on a job that you desperately want to keep. Time is moving so slowly that you think you'll explode.*

On the job, you might want to share your stress with a friend who's willing to help distract you while you wait. Ask your friend, "Will you tell me how wonderful I am no matter how my evaluation comes out? I need your support now."

▶ *You are the happiest you have ever been in your whole life; you're successful at work, surrounded by your family, and in great health. You feel as if there is nothing that you can't do.*

Enjoy the process of living, while being aware of false expectations. Remember, we are all human with strengths and vulnerabilities. When you are happy, enjoy it thoroughly. When times change, know that you will be able to adapt.

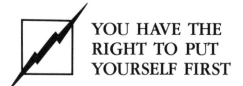

YOU HAVE THE RIGHT TO PUT YOURSELF FIRST

Our first job in life is to be responsible for ourselves. Each of us can only effectively take care of our own behaviors, feelings, and general well-being. Each of us can do these jobs better than anyone else because we know best what we like and dislike.

It's important to take care of ourselves first in our lives, because only when we have accomplished this are we available to take care of others. After all, in airplanes we are instructed to first put the oxygen mask on our own faces before putting one on our child's. Life is the same.

Others see us as models. And by caring for ourselves first, we show them that it is important to value ourselves. Show others a first-class product.

YOU'VE GOT THE POWER

Sometimes it is necessary to safeguard your status when others jeopardize it through their words or actions. They may accuse you of being selfish, of only thinking of yourself. Respond by saying, "Yes, I take responsibility for myself." They may tell you what you should do. Or they may discount your worth by ignoring your limits, telling you what you should be feeling or how you ought to act. Say, "That's what *you* feel. I feel differently." At other times you may find that people are trying to enhance their own status at the expense of yours. You have the right to neutralize their efforts. The best way is to bring the situation out in the open.

WHAT TO DO AND SAY

▶   *A colleague presents a team project to the boss as his or her own idea.*

At work, clarify in your mind what really has happened in a situation where someone takes advantage of you. Stay calm and say, "I can't let you do that." Or, look incredulously at your colleague and say, "I don't understand why you told people that was your project. Please explain it to me. I also need you to clarify it to the boss."

▶   *A friend goes out with someone else after making plans to go out with you. This is the second time it has happened.*

In personal relationships you can say, "I don't deserve to be treated poorly. I'll back off until I feel better about our relationship."

▶   *You turn down an invitation only to find yourself pressured to attend and accused of being a party pooper.*

When you want to take care of yourself and others won't leave you alone, say, "Don't pressure me. I'll come when I want to." If you are told you are a party pooper, say, "That's what you think. I think differently." You might end with a teasing remark, "Now get on out of here. This is my time you're intruding on." Keeping it light will help you keep your friends and take care of yourself.

 ## GIVE YOURSELF CREDIT FOR HAVING GROWN

When something unsettling happens, you may upset yourself more than you need to because you're comparing your current problem with one in the past. You fear that same negative outcome this time.

"If the problem is this bad now, how is it ever going to get better so that I'll get what I want?"

It may feel like you've been in this situation before and it didn't improve with time. Or you felt you weren't able to handle it then and now you feel like panicking. But before you run out of the room or the relationship, you need to remember that

you will meet your own needs. If something or someone seems to stand in your way, know that it's an illusion. You will meet your goals, personally and professionally, but you may not do it in the same way or in the same amount of time as others. Timing is crucial here because what you may see as an obstacle or setback is really what's appropriate for you right now. When it does happen, you will know you're ready for it.

YOU'VE GOT THE POWER

When you're honest with yourself, you will know when you're in an unworkable situation and need to get out. Otherwise,

- ☐ Reassure yourself that you've made a better choice this time.

- ☐ Blank out all thoughts of the past and future and concentrate on this moment.

- ☐ Say, "No matter what anyone else does or says, I will get what I need."

WHAT TO DO AND SAY

▶ *Your boss doesn't believe in your abilities and is reluctant to grant you increased responsibilities.*

When an opportunity presents itself, say to your boss, "I know I'm ready for more responsibility." Resist the easy temptation to display cynicism and bitterness. Continue to do a good job and look for chances where you can show your skills.

▶ *Your spouse spends too much money. You've already been through one bankruptcy and don't want another.*

Tell your spouse your worries. Say, "I've been in a situation similar to this before. It led to a disastrous bankruptcy and I'm concerned this will, too. Could we talk about some ways we can stop this now so I'll feel better and you'll be happy?"

▶   *You're afraid for your child's future because she is a discipline problem now.*

Rejoice that your child speaks out and acts like an individual because it's a sign of an independent mind. Encourage her to have her own opinions and ask often how you can help her get what she needs. Social dropouts rarely receive any of this support.

 **TRUST YOURSELF**

There is no one in the world who knows what you need and want better than you do. Your intuition or gut level feeling about these things is one of the major guideposts you have. Intuition provides information through your feelings instead of your thoughts. There is nothing magical about it. Men and women alike have it, but are often unaware of it. If you do not *feel* trusting of yourself, however, it is because you were taught not to trust yourself when you were a child. Every child is intuitive and feels confident until taught differently.

If we were abused or neglected as children, we learned to distrust our feelings. It may have been unintentional, but nevertheless, abuse or neglect was the culprit. There is no way that a rational mind can make sense of someone we trust hurting us. For emotional protection, we learned to distrust our own judgment and instead figured that we must not be seeing things the way they really are. This may have led us to discount other feelings until a general distrust of ourselves set in.

As an adult, you can now believe in yourself. In fact, you have a responsibility to take charge of yourself again. And you will find that no one knows as well as you do what you need, or the way in which you like it delivered. You *can* trust your judgments about yourself.

YOU'VE GOT THE POWER

If you were or are a victim of abuse, get some professional help to teach you how to re-contact your true self. Then, reawaken belief in yourself by learning to listen to your intuition. Intuition is made up of your feelings. It's often experienced as a little voice in the back of your mind or a strange feeling in the pit of your stomach.

☐ Trust your intuition a little at a time. You might want to begin in a social situation that isn't very important in your life. When you are involved in a group of people, notice which ones you are attracted to and which ones you tend to back away from. Then give yourself permission to go toward those you like and see if you don't have a better time with and receive better treatment from these people than you have in the past.

☐ Later, as your belief in yourself builds, take on bigger challenges, such as looking for a new job when you feel your boss is being overbearing. Know there is nothing wrong with you but rather with your boss. Trust your judgment.

☐ When you prefer to do things differently from others, it is not necessary to put them down or to give up the way you do things. Instead, acknowledge and respect your differences and expect them to do the same. Believe in what feels right for you even when *experts* set the guidelines.

WHAT TO DO AND SAY

▶ *You beat yourself up emotionally, when someone criticizes the way you do things.*

When someone criticizes you, visualize yourself as a small child. Comfort and protect that child and let him/her know you will not also beat up on that child part of you. Then say supportive things like, "I'll take care of you. You do the best you can do. Your way is just fine for me."

▶ *You try to fit into the styles presented by the latest advertising even though you aren't very comfortable with them.*

Whenever you find yourself uncomfortable with the latest trends, simply give yourself permission to be different, saying, "It's okay to be who I am, liking what I like. I like my uniqueness." In doing so, you may start a trend of your own.

▶ *You feel uneasy because you really don't like to be competitive, but others tell you it's the only way to get ahead.*

When someone offers a generalization, allow yourself the privilege of staying outside of it. Say to someone who tells you that being competitive is the only way to get ahead, "I'm glad being competitive works for you, but it's not something I value as highly. I appreciate your concern, but I prefer to do things my way." It's especially hard to maintain your position when others seem to be progressing while you are not. But stay true to yourself. Your time will come.

PEOPLE SHOW THEY CARE IN DIFFERENT WAYS

There is no one correct definition of love. Everyone knows the feeling, but it may be expressed in different ways and still mean the same.

If you feel that no one around you loves you, then sit down and figure out what you think love means. If it's solely connected to the actions of others, you may be hung up on having people *prove* that they love you rather than just accepting that they do.

Abuse is never love. But neglect may be. Neglect doesn't always signify the absence of love. So if someone does not spend enough time with you or give you what you want, she may be short on time, not managing her schedule well, or working on something that doesn't involve you. You can ask for more time but you may be pressuring her to give you the love you need to be giving yourself.

If you think there truly isn't anyone who loves you, it could be a reflection of your own lack of self-love.

YOU'VE GOT THE POWER

Instead of focusing on whether your partner loves you or not, look at how you feel about yourself.

- ☐ Get in touch with the little child within you who still needs to be nurtured and protected.

- ☐ Take a few minutes and give that child love and reassurance that it is lovable.

- ☐ Visualize yourself in a beautiful place of security and peace with your child in your arms.

- ☐ Give your child a hug and a reminder that you will always love and cherish it. That no matter who comes and goes in your life, you will always be there for it.

Try this every time you're feeling unloved. You'll be amazed at how good you will feel and how much other people will notice the difference in you. You'll also be able to love people for who they are and not for what they can do for you.

WHAT TO DO AND SAY

▶ *A friend hasn't called for a week and you
think he doesn't like you anymore.*

If someone you care about is neglecting you, call him
up and say, "I've really missed you lately. Do you
have some time that we could spend together?" If
he's involved in something else or just says no, wish
him well and ask him to get in touch with you when
he's free. Then let go.

▶ *Your spouse spends more time with your
young child than you.*

Hire a babysitter for a night or a weekend away so
that you and your spouse can have more time together. Reassure her that the child will be okay. So
will both of you with a little attention. Emphasize
how much you really want her company.

SOMEONE CAN LOVE
YOU AND STILL
FORGET

Have you ever wondered why your partner can remember Larry Bird's rebound average or how many
calories a dish has, but can't remember your birthday, or to pick up the dry cleaning after work? You

may be involved with someone who does not have an efficient memory.

YOU'VE GOT THE POWER

Forgetting an important event doesn't mean someone doesn't care about you. Your partner may not be as in touch with his feelings as you are and may need help translating his feelings into action. Or your wife may have come from a family that didn't emphasize celebrating holidays, birthdays, or anniversaries, and she may never attach the same importance to the anniversary of your first date as you do.

What's important is whether you're in a power struggle over it. What sometimes happens is that one of you *deliberately* forgets in order to gain some control—or even some revenge. You know: "He forgot my birthday. Now it's *his* turn to see how it feels . . ." Resist that temptation. It never helps. Instead, communicate how you feel about the situation, then ask him what he intends to do. When he sees the hurt his forgetfulness caused, he's sure to do better next time.

WHAT TO SAY AND DO

▶ *Your wife forgets to tape your favorite TV program for you.*

Let her know how important this is to you. Ask her if there's any way you can help with reminders.

▶ *He forgets your wedding anniversary.*

Don't lose your temper. If he loves you, he didn't do it on purpose. Ask: "Did you intend to hurt my feelings?" You may find a lot of your hurt soothed over by just that simple "No." Help him to remember by marking significant dates on his daily planner or calendar.

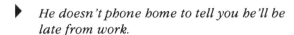

▶　*He doesn't phone home to tell you he'll be late from work.*

Choose a good time when he feels comfortable and not defensive, and explain to him how frightened you feel when he doesn't call. Ask him to put out more effort to let you know when he'll be late. Make sure he realizes that it's not that you don't trust him—it's just that you worry about his safety.

THERE ARE NO PERFECT PEOPLE

Often, when we see people who have an outstanding or unusual talent, we tend to view them as heroes or saints—as if everything they do is at that same outstanding level. It is also not unusual for high status to be confused with being exceptional in all things. The creative artist, however, may not be able to balance a checkbook. The scientific genius may have poor people skills, or the CEO may be able to manage the company but not the kids.

No one is perfect. Oftentimes, you only see what that person or the media allows you to see. And, let's face it, most people do not choose to have their imperfections displayed. Devoid of makeup, caught under stress, or thrown into situations that require them to function in their areas of weakness, they all appear only human.

No one can be perfect, or be all things to all people all the time. If you are trying to, realize that your perfectionism came about as an attempt to avoid criticism and win approval as a child. You can learn differently because you can now be safe whether you perform perfectly or not.

YOU'VE GOT THE POWER

Each of us has strengths and weaknesses. Make a list of yours, being cautious to sort out what you can do from what you think you should be able to do.

☐ Go over your list carefully and decide what you already excel at. Compliment yourself on how well you do in those areas, and draw strength from that knowledge. Say, "I'm just right exactly as I am."

☐ If you were embarrassed or hurt while learning as a child, realize that your parents and teachers did not understand *how* you learned or what you wanted to learn. They undoubtedly held up models of perfection for you to follow that were an illusion—*their* illusion. Forgive them and go on realizing that you are wonderful, just as you are. Most important, forgive yourself for not being able to learn in the way other people wanted you to learn. Then say, "Thank you" to yourself for learning in the way you do learn.

☐ If you find an area in which you want to improve, set realistic goals for your improvement campaign and break that campaign down into manageable steps. Go about the learning process the way you like best. Some people like going to a teacher or a class. Others like to learn by themselves proceeding one step at a time. Say, "I can do it," or "Learning is fun."

☐ Make a list of your vulnerabilities and weaknesses; then give yourself permission to exist with them without losing self-esteem. Teach yourself to work around them.

☐ Reject, kindly, the accolades of others who try to make you seem perfect.

WHAT TO DO AND SAY

▶ *You read about a Woman of the Year award and feel inferior.*

Realize that a Woman of the Year is only a symbol for the millions of deserving women, one of whom is you. The particular woman who won has assets and liabilities, just like you. You just know yours better than you know hers. Say to yourself, "I'm as deserving as she."

▶ *You compare your lovemaking to that of a star in a movie and feel inadequate.*

Remember that if you got paid, had a script, and were acting, you'd look like a great lover, too. Say, "I'm open to being human in my relationships and will continue to learn about sex."

▶ *You don't feel you are smart because you didn't make good grades in school.*

In school, only certain kinds of intellectual skills are showcased. Your strengths probably lay in other areas that you may not have had the opportunity to develop. Make a list of your assets. Feel proud of yourself.

▶ *You have certain talents that have catapulted you into the public eye. Others expect you to be equally good at everything.*

Recognize that you are human, like everyone else. Keep your humility and refuse to get caught up in the mania of public opinion that expects you to be superior. Say, "Yes, I have certain skills," "but I also have my weaknesses." You don't need to drag your weaknesses out, parading them ostentatiously, but don't deny them either.

MARRIAGE WON'T MAKE ANYONE PERFECT

Many people have a heartbreaking expectation about marriage, that it's like a magic wand that will make a spouse perfect—like they never were before the marriage. While you're dating, you overlook those little things that would ordinarily annoy you. You're in love, all's well with the world—what are a few irritating habits between soulmates? Heartbreaking, because it's only found to be false after the ceremony, and now you're stuck—at least until the divorce. Some people go through marriage after marriage, waiting for that magic wand, when the real truth is what they had before they made it legal may have been the best they were going to get.

Marriage vows are a statement of commitment, not an incantation of perfection. Most people are on their best behavior when they're dating—they have a goal, to meet a marriage partner, and they give their top performances to achieve that goal. Once they get married, then they often relax and revert to their true selves. Your husband must love you the way you are or he wouldn't have married you, right? Unfortunately, he may never have seen the person you really are. And if you spent your courtship trying to change him, you will spend your marriage doing the same thing.

What's most important is to look at the other person very clearly while you're dating. This way you won't be disappointed when you discover that your spouse is only human after the ceremony.

YOU'VE GOT THE POWER

It's amazing what you can discover the first time you compare notes on what's important to each of you and how that will affect whether you want to spend the rest of your lives together.

Realize there are no perfect people. Look at how you get along and in what ways you don't. Decide if you can live with the things that annoy you because they probably won't go away and if the things that delight you about the person outweigh the drawbacks.

WHAT TO DO AND SAY

▶ *You and he fight every time an important issue comes up but you believe you'll live "happily ever after" anyway.*

After you've thought about the plusses and minuses of your partner, sit down and tell him what you really love about him. Then say, "But there are some areas that I'm concerned about. We don't seem to think about money in the same way." As you're discussing the important issues, ask your partner what he likes about you and has any fears about. This could lead to a higher degree of trust between the two of you.

▶ *You resent the time he spends with his friends but think he'll give them up after the wedding.*

Ask, "If you want to see as much of your friends after we're married, can we discuss how we'll find time to spend with each other?"

▶ *You aren't getting your emotional needs met, but you still think your partner will "open up" once the marriage is secure.*

Stress the positive. Say, "I really enjoy it when you pay attention to me," "I feel wonderful when you say 'I love you,'" or "I like it when you hug me for no reason." Realize that your partner may have come from a family that wasn't verbally or physically affectionate. Time and experience on his part and encouragement and patience on yours may make the difference. If you need more help, see a marriage counselor with your partner or go by yourself.

SEX IS NEVER SIMPLE

There is a myth around that sex is something people will automatically know how to do, that it is easy, and that if love between the partners is strong enough, it will simply work well. Another myth tells us that if we are feminine or masculine enough, we will automatically be wonderful in bed. Not necessarily so.

It really doesn't matter whether you are talking about first-time sex or sex at seventy. Every sexual encounter can seem like a first-time experience, even with the same partner. This is because each of us continually changes as we go through daily living. Although you are more likely to feel nervous if you haven't had sexual relations for a while, no one can breeze through a sexual encounter without communicating needs and wishes. From that communication real intimacy grows.

Learning to read each other's needs is difficult. Overcoming old programming that has taught us inhibitions or restrictions takes time. Discovering that sex is not a performance but a communication of feelings takes a lot of trust from both partners.

In addition, all kinds of feelings and circumstances get in the way of enjoyable sex: anger, resentment, fear, fatigue, emotional overload, grief, small children, change, and creative projects. Sex is often the first thing that goes in a relationship and the last thing to come back to normal during times of stress. So, please, be kind to yourself and your partner. Don't expect to share your sexuality easily, or that every encounter should be earthshaking.

YOU'VE GOT THE POWER

When you want to make love with your partner, communicate your wish.

☐ Then ask your partner what is pleasing to him. Give to and ask for feedback from the other person so that you can learn about each other.

☐ NEVER, NEVER let anyone do anything to you that you don't like or want. Sex is to be enjoyed. It is not a power play. It is not a situation where *shoulds* have any place. No matter what, remember you only have power in relation to yourself in the sexual arena. You have no power over another.

☐ And, most important of all, remember that sex is to be enjoyed. You don't have to prove anything.

WHAT TO DO AND SAY

▶ *You and your spouse recently packed your last child off to college and are ready to spend your first night alone together in years.*

Be honest with yourself. If you are nervous, talk to yourself and say, "Of course I am nervous. I care about my spouse." Explain your feelings to your spouse, who may be feeling the same way. Then place your focus on the present situation and reassure yourself, saying, "I am a loving person. I give myself permission to enjoy this new freedom with my spouse after all this time. I plan to enjoy myself and to give enjoyment. And each of us has the power to say 'no' to anything that we don't like or enjoy."

▶ *Your divorce is now final and you are ready to date again. There's a special person to whom you are attracted, but your only sexual experience has been with your ex. You are feeling scared.*

Be aware of your timing. Don't let anyone rush you. It's okay to pull away if you begin to feel unsafe, and it's okay to communicate these feelings with your partner. If your partner continues to pressure you, remember you don't "owe" this person anything you are not willing to give.

▶   *Your marriage is riddled with anger and resentment, and you find you are not attracted to your spouse anymore.*

Anger and resentment create large barriers to sexual enjoyment. To your partner, say, "I am too angry to want to have sex with you. We'll need to work on other things first." If you don't choose to communicate with your partner or try to solve the problems, be aware of this, and the possible repercussions to the relationship. But do not confuse your emotional condition with a lack of sexuality in yourself. Rather, think of your sexuality as being in storage until you choose to get it out.

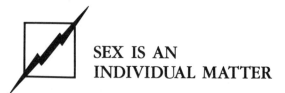

SEX IS AN INDIVIDUAL MATTER

Sex *isn't* simple, but you don't have to make it more complex than it already is. Each of us has a natural capacity for intimacy until it is disturbed by being hurt or by being taught that we *should* feel or act in a certain way. It is imperative that you tune into your own feelings and separate what you feel from what others say and do. Leave generalizations behind.

Some common myths about sex that you need to ignore, especially in the heat of passion, include:

For women: "Men don't like to wear condoms."

"Men need more sex than women."

"This is the way to *really* make sex fulfilling."

For men: "Women don't like sex as much as men."

"Women don't think you are special unless you spend a lot of money on them first."

"Women don't like to experiment."

Don't believe generalizations about the opposite sex, such as:

All men/women can't be trusted.

All men are after is your body.

All women like to be pushed when they say, "no."

Generalizations about *all* men or *all* women aren't worth anything. Each one of us is unique, as is every relationship. It is up to the couple to develop a union that is comfortable for both of them. There should be no winners or losers.

YOU'VE GOT THE POWER

Don't let anyone make you feel guilty about sexual issues in order to get you to do something you don't want to do. Tell your partner if you are uncomfortable with what he wants to do, and if your partner persists, say, "No."

☐   If your partner says, "You got me aroused, now you must go all the way with me." Say, "I didn't mean to make you so uncomfortable, and I'm not ready to go any farther. Please respect my wishes." Be definite.

☐   If necessary, get tough and say, "It's okay for you to be angry, but I'm not doing anything that doesn't feel right to me, and if you can't accept that perhaps we should rethink this relationship."

WHAT TO DO AND SAY

▶   *A new boyfriend tells you not to be silly about wanting to protect yourself against pregnancy. He says it's safe.*

When your partner doesn't want to use a condom, say, "I don't want to take a chance on becoming pregnant. I'm not willing to make love with you unless you use a condom."

▶   *You just lost your job and feel you need to prove yourself by finding someone to love you.*

Sex is not a remedy for all ills. When you're upset about losing your job, tell yourself that's a separate issue. Get support in other ways while you look for another job. Say, "I am valuable, whether I have a job or not. I am lovable whether I have a job or not."

▶ *You are told you* should *enjoy a particular sexual maneuver, and you feel guilty about letting your partner down when you say you don't enjoy it.*

Watch Out for controlling behavior in the area of sex.

When someone says, "What's wrong with you? You should be *enjoying* this," say, "Nothing is wrong with me, and I don't enjoy it, so let's try something else."

When someone says, "This is the right way to make love," you can say, "The right way is what *both* of us enjoy."

When someone tells you, "You will get used to doing this even though you don't like it now," you can say, "I love you, but I'm not willing to 'get used to' this."

LIFE IS A SERIES OF PROBLEM-SOLVING EVENTS

Have you ever noticed that the minute you solve one problem, there is another one to take its place? Rarely does a day go by without several challenges to keep life interesting.

If you're waiting for a problem-free time to enjoy yourself or waiting for some goal to be reached before you have any fun, you're likely to feel frustrated. Problem-free times rarely occur and do not last long. This has to do with the nature of our problem-solving capability: We tend to see or focus on situations that cause us to be unbalanced or incomplete. If you try to get all the pieces of your life balanced at once, like getting the four legs of a table even, you'll want to pull your hair out.

Whether you experience life as negative or positive will depend a lot on how you look at the job of solving your particular array of problems. If you consider solving problems as a game or a challenge, you can make life fun.

See life as a process. By flowing from one event to another, you can teach yourself to live in the process rather than waiting for a goal to be reached. That way you enjoy every moment.

YOU'VE GOT THE POWER

Consider life as a series of problem-solving events. Set your mind in order so that you can have some fun with the process of solving those problems. When you get up in the morning, ask yourself with enthusiasm, "I wonder what problems I'll get to solve today."

- ☐ Look forward to the surprise element that each day holds and you won't be caught off guard.

- ☐ Focus on each problem for itself and give it your full attention. Rather than fighting it, wrap yourself around it and thank it for being there to provide you with mental exercise.

- ☐ Congratulate yourself at the end of each day as you review the individual problems that you have solved.

- ☐ And finally, laugh a lot.

WHAT TO DO AND SAY

▶ *You are waiting until you finish graduate
school before you give yourself time to enjoy
the simple things in life.*

Plan some fun time regularly. It's up to you to take
charge and set limits on your production. There is
always more work that can fill in your time. Say, "I
commit to x hours daily (or weekly) to do with as
I wish." Don't let anything get in the way.

▶ *You no sooner get one of your children settled
down than the next one needs your attention.*

With children, realize you are dealing with a situation that does not have an end. The teaching process
with kids can be exciting if you don't let yourself get
overly tense and serious about every small problem.
Fortunately for parents, kids tend to take turns in
their need for attention. Get your respite by carving
out time for yourself regularly, and assure yourself
that it will all work out in the long run.

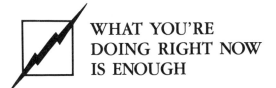

WHAT YOU'RE DOING RIGHT NOW IS ENOUGH

It's amazing how even total strangers will ask you
what you plan to do in the future as if what you're
doing right now doesn't count. It's important to set

goals and have dreams, but the true key to happiness lies in your satisfaction with what you are doing right now. It's easy to get thrown off track by others' insistence or implications that what you are doing now pales in comparison to what you want or plan to do in the future.

Since you move at the pace that best suits you, you don't have to justify yourself to anyone. Life is not about getting to your next destination—it's about enjoying the sights along the way.

YOU'VE GOT THE POWER

There will always be people who will try to judge your ability to live your life the way they think you should. Some are deliberately malicious but many just don't know any better. Remember to protect yourself from all of them.

- ☐ Say to yourself, "I am content with what I'm doing, and how I am working towards my dreams for the future." Since this person has no business asking such personal questions, you can choose to reply or not. Although people can be very rude, you don't have to react in the same way. It is perfectly polite to say, "This is not a subject I care to discuss anymore."

WHAT TO DO AND SAY

▶ *Someone asks you when you'll be getting a "better" job—say, as a manager.*

"I'm working towards that but I'm happy with what I'm doing right now."

▶   *You're not married or even dating, and someone wants to know when you will be.*

Just say, "I'm very happy as I am" or "When I'm ready, the right person will come along, but I'm doing great just as it is now."

▶   *You don't have children, and people ask when you plan to have them.*

"We've talked about it, but right now we're happy as we are." If you don't plan to have any children, say so.

YOU'VE GOT TO ASK FOR WHAT YOU WANT

There is a great tendency for many of us to think that others can read our minds, knowing what we need and want. People say things like,

"If you really loved me, you would know what I want."

"You've been with me for such a long time that I'm sure you know what I need."

"I would give you such and such if you were in *my* situation, so I assumed you would give it to me."

Assuming that another person knows what you

want without you telling them is useless. You can't assume that past history or love will give someone the ability to know what you are thinking or needing. Believing that others will act the same way you would is also setting yourself up for trouble.

YOU'VE GOT THE POWER

Be clear in your mind what it is that you feel. Figure out what you need in order to feel better.

☐ Translate that need into a request in your mind.

☐ Select the person you want to fulfill your need.

☐ Make an "I want" request.

Many people believe they are making an "I want" statement when, in reality, they are not. "Don't you want to go out to dinner?" or "It would be nice to go out tonight" are quite different from "I want us to go out tonight."

The problem, of course, in saying "I want" is that you may get a negative response. But you may also get a "yes" response. Regardless of the response, your request will be clear and you will know you have done all you can do to get your needs met by another person. You'll then be free to meet your own unmet needs yourself.

Sometimes a trade-off is a good negotiation tool to get what you want. You might say, "I'm tired, I know you are, too. I'll give you a back rub if you'll give me one."

WHAT TO DO AND SAY

▶ *You arrive home, tired from work, and assume your spouse knows that you want to go out to dinner.*

Talk about your feelings to your spouse. Say, "I'm really tired. Let's go out to dinner."

▶ *You fail to tell your boss that she is giving you too much work for you to do a good job and not get burned out.*

Say to her, "To do a good job for you, I want you to set priorities for which jobs you want me to complete first." If you know it's a practical request, ask for an assistant.

▶ *You always offer to listen when a friend is feeling down, but when you're down, your friend doesn't reciprocate.*

When you expect a friend to treat you the same way you treat her in a similar situation, and it doesn't happen, stop and ask for what you want. Don't assume. Say, "Will you listen to me today? I feel down." If your friend continuously fails to respond, so that you have to ask every time, say, "I automatically listen when you're down. Do you realize I want you to do the same?" You may discover your friend simply cannot be a listener. Then, listen to her only *if* you want to. In the meantime, focus on what else you do have in common, and seek out friends who can listen to you when you need it.

TAKE RESPONSIBILITY FOR SOLVING YOUR OWN PROBLEMS

How many times have you said to someone, "I have a problem," and expected him or her to solve it for you? Perhaps decision-making is difficult for you. But expecting others to find solutions for you excludes you from an important growth process: learning to take responsibility for your own life.

By relying on other people you give away your power. Even if a problem is solved, you may feel helpless because your actions are directed by someone else. If a problem isn't solved, you may even blame those people who tried to help you. Even if you don't, people may feel resentful because they want to help but they don't want to make your decisions for you.

Or you may be able to identify a problem but not follow through on finding a solution. Congratulate yourself on understanding what the problem is, and then start identifying your options. The options you see may not offer you the answers you need, but are valuable starting points from which to brainstorm about other possibilities—either by yourself or with friends who may offer useful ideas of their own. But *you* decide on your course of action. And without that extra burden of possible blame, your friends or family will be more likely to want to help you in the future even if things don't work out the way you want.

YOU'VE GOT THE POWER

Acknowledge to yourself that no one knows what you need better than you do. And tell yourself that you are strong enough to take responsibility for running your own life.

☐ Begin with identifying one problem at a time.

☐ Examine your options. Resolve to come up with at least one solution, no matter how far-fetched.

☐ Check out the free hot lines that are staffed by people who have been trained to help others.

☐ Explain your problem to a friend, outline your thoughts on it, and ask if he has any ideas.

☐ Acknowledge that whatever decision you make is *your* decision, and not anyone else's.

WHAT TO DO AND SAY

▶ *You can't get your job done at work and have to sit down with the boss about it.*

If you start with the word "problem" as you sit down with your boss, he may think you want him to figure it out. So start with: "I'm having difficulty with _____," (or "I'm finding it hard to _____,") "but I could do my job better if we tried _____." It will help your boss if you've already thought about your solution, and makes it easier to go from there to see what other options might work.

> ▶ *Your child is doing poorly in school and you feel you've tried everything.*

Tell your child that you are on her side and will help in any way you can. Don't accuse her of not trying and don't expect her to know what is wrong. Ask your child for suggestions, then join in with a brainstorming session. Present it to the school. Do ask for help from the principal if you're not satisfied, but don't make the teacher out to be a bad guy. Your child may still have to be in the same class. If you're still frustrated, seek out professional help in your child's area of difficulty and get their suggestions.

> ▶ *You want to stop being dependent on a loved one but you still ask for or accept their help.*

Most times, loved ones help you as an expression of their love. This makes their help difficult to decline. Seldom do they realize that the control they exert may actually inhibit your growth. Say, "I have to be free to make my own decisions now, and free to make my own mistakes." Then define the kind of help you are willing to accept. Say "I love you and appreciate your wish to help, but what I need from you is just a willing listener (or advice)." Then thank them and say, "Once I have made my decision, I'll be glad to let you know what it is."

STAY IN CONTROL WITH CONTROLLING PEOPLE

Some people want everyone and everything under their control. They want to tell you what to do, and how to do it . . . even though you are grown and perfectly capable. They want you to do things their way . . . even though there's nothing wrong with *your* way.

They get angry or resentful or have hurt feelings when you don't want to do things their way. They put you down verbally or psychologically, because they feel you are taking away their power if you don't let them make decisions for you.

Frequently, controlling people invoke their belief system to reinforce their being in control. They believe you *should* do what they want you to do because it is the *right* thing according to their belief. You need to realize that controlling people judge, blame, and discount you to get what they want when they want it. You do not have to go along with their agendas.

YOU'VE GOT THE POWER

Try to be patient, but definitely be firm when dealing with a controlling person. Talk evenly, softly, and a bit slowly.

Under NO circumstances should you give in to the pressure exerted by the controlling person. When you do, you reinforce that person's power over you.

And, don't express anger and resentment. Instead, calm yourself and walk away. Or say, "I'll be back when we each are in better control of ourselves." Then leave.

WHAT TO DO AND SAY

▶ *Your boss finds it impossible to give you an assignment and then let go of control, demanding you do the job* his *way.*

While believing that you have a right to be in control of yourself, say to your boss, "I appreciate your advice, but since you've given me the responsibility for this project, let me try it my way. Let's meet in a week's time and I'll give you a progress report."

▶ *Your spouse becomes angry when you don't do a household chore the way she wants you to and in the time frame she wants.*

At home, say to your spouse, "Each of us has our own way of doing this and I've allocated the time I need for it." If your spouse gets angry, suggest she go have a cup of coffee and say that you'll talk about your differences when she's calmer. In the meantime, continue to do it your way.

▶ *Your controlling parent wanted you to* want *to make good grades and enjoy the "thrill" of learning.*

When your parents continue to try to control you, say, "What I'm doing is not *against* you, but *for* myself. I'm choosing to make good grades because it will get me ahead in life, but I don't have to like it. I realize *you* love the thrill of learning but I don't. I hope you'll love me anyway. I love you."

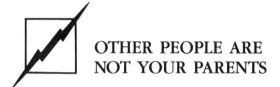

OTHER PEOPLE ARE NOT YOUR PARENTS

Once again, you find yourself in a struggle with someone because they want to tell you how to run your life. Either you withdraw and say only to yourself what you'd like to say to the other person, or you raise your voice and still don't get your message across. If this seems all too familiar, it may be because it's the same way you fought with your parents when *they* were too critical. Others may own some of the same traits as your mom or dad. That may be why you were attracted to them in the first place: to try and win the battles with your parents that you never did as a child.

First, remember this: other people are not your parents and you are not a child anymore. That seems obvious, but it's a truth we often forget in personal interaction.

Second, look at the criticisms you are now receiving apart from the criticisms you received in the past. Then judge the criticisms on their own merits. If there is anything valid, you might want to act on it. Sometimes we resist changes that could be good for us because we're trying to protect the child within us from hurts in the past.

YOU'VE GOT THE POWER

Some of the signs that the critical messages from your parents are being triggered might be: You feel trapped and helpless/want to withdraw/can only say what you need to in your head/want to yell at the other person so they will back off or just leave.

☐ Reflect back to the child within you who didn't know how to protect himself or herself from criticism. Offer your child comfort.

☐ Acknowledge your ability to take care of yourself now.

☐ See clearly the person who is criticizing you now. Recognize that this person is not your parent.

☐ Now, objectively examine the present criticism.

WHAT TO DO AND SAY

▶ *You feel angry because someone close to you is always putting you down.*

Say to your friend or relative, calmly, "You seem to be upset with something I've done. Could you tell me what you need from me so I can help you get it?"

▶ *You're locked in a power struggle with your boss.*

See if your boss's criticisms or suggestions have any merit. You could ask, "Can I think about these ideas for a while and get back to you?" If they're trivial changes that differ every week, your boss may be looking for approval or seeking assurance that his or her authority over you is intact. Take a notepad in, write a few things down, nod your head a lot, smile, and then follow through on *some* of the suggestions, even if they are trivial. At the next meeting, find a reason to ask for advice.

▶ *You don't want to listen to a friend's suggestions.*

Say to your friend, "Thanks for your advice. I'm glad you care enough to be concerned. I hope I can come to you for advice when I do need it." Then change the subject.

TRUST . . . BUT NOT EVERYONE ALL THE TIME

Though it might be quite nice to live in a world that contains 100%-trustworthy people and in which events were predictable, we don't. Wearing rose-colored glasses can set you up for a whole lot of pain. Expecting others to always be there for you is expecting too much even from people who really do care about you. Expecting your plans to work out as anticipated ignores Murphy's Law, which states that anything that can go wrong, will.

This state of affairs is not a cause for depression or resentment. It just means that you need to be realistic in your expectations.

Often the problem materializes when we move too quickly into an intense situation with a person or a new project. Not knowing what the limits are, and not having enough information, may make you unreasonably optimistic. But people cannot be held responsible because we *want* them to be more than what they can be.

YOU'VE GOT THE POWER

Assess each situation you are a part of with regard to the responsibility of the people with whom you are involved. Ask yourself, "What can I reasonably expect?" See if those reasonable expectations are being met.

☐   Check on the reliability of those with whom you do business. It is common practice and quite acceptable to check references or get input from colleagues and friends when beginning an association with someone new.

☐   If a person lets you down, expect him to volunteer a plausible explanation. If he does not, then ask for one. If a second letdown occurs, begin to be suspicious. Do not set yourself up for repeated failure with a person or situation that is simply not working for you.

☐ Be sure to see what is really happening rather than what you want to see. Be honest with yourself.

☐ Have a backup plan that makes use of other people, routes and strategies for reaching your goal, should there be a change from what you anticipate.

☐ It's okay to trust, just don't expect too much.

WHAT TO DO AND SAY

▶ *Your best friend yells at you when all you were trying to do was help. You feel hurt and misunderstood.*

When your best friend yells at you, say, "I didn't mean to hit a sore spot. Please tell me what happened." Then listen, and see if there is anything you can do to help.

▶ *You set a delivery date for a job to be ready based on a promise from a supplier. You didn't get your material on time and you can't meet the delivery date.*

Tell your customer the truth. Say, "I'm sorry, I can't get your order to you as I promised. My supplier didn't come through." Then say what you do have the power to deliver and how you plan to remedy the situation.

▶ *You invite your new neighbor to stop by for a
chat "anytime." Anytime has become every
day and he insists on telling you all his problems. You begin to dread every knock at your
door.*

Realize that you do not have the power to solve this
person's problems and that you do have a right to
your privacy.

The next time he appears, say, "I'm busy right now
and don't have time for a visit."

The next time, say, "I only have fifteen minutes to
spare." Somewhere within his monologue interject,
"I can't solve your problems for you. You might want
to see a counselor." At the end of that time, say,
"Well, I must get back to work now, so I'm afraid
you'll have to leave."

As you wean this person from his dependency,
resolve to be more cautious in offering your friendship to people you do not know.

NOBODY LIKES TO LISTEN TO CRITICISM

Telling a person, "You are wrong," or asking, "Why
don't you do _____ anymore?" will usually provoke
one of three reactions:

(1) He'll get mad, shut down, and only hear his own
voice saying, "No, you're wrong, I'm right."

(2) She'll use what you've said as a club to beat herself up with: "I really am a useless person, I can't do anything right."

(3) He'll blow up, you'll end up fighting about everything except the original subject, and someone will go stomping out the door.

Whatever the response, you're wasting your breath and time because no one is going to hear what you're saying.

YOU'VE GOT THE POWER

When you feel the need to criticize, keep the conversation positive. Talk about what you appreciate about that person, how you value what he or she does, and say that you want to see more of it in the future. Concentrate on saying what you want instead of what you don't want.

☐ Rather than using a lot of negative "You" or "Why" sentences, such as, "You aren't doing your share," "You're doing it wrong," or "Why can't you be like _____?," change them to positive "I" sentences: "I'd like you to do more of _____," "I'd like you to try it this way," or "I'd like you to be _____."

☐ Next, talk about your feelings. "I'm upset because of _____" or "I'm really sad that _____ didn't happen." Then ask how you can help that person to do what needs to be done.

WHAT TO DO AND SAY

▶ *You are frustrated with an employee, but your criticism so far has only made him hostile.*

Try saying, "I've always appreciated your hard work and how you get your projects done on time. Lately I've noticed it's been tougher for you. Is there anything I can do to help you?"

▶ *Your spouse doesn't send flowers anymore, even though you complain.*

In the case of flowers or other romantic gestures, say, "You've sent me flowers before and I really liked them. Would you send me them again?" You could also try, "Yesterday I was thinking about the time you sent me flowers at work, and how happy I was, and how it made my whole week. I just wanted to thank you for them again and tell you how much I love you." Then let it go. Everyone loves compliments and appreciation and will always try harder for those who give them.

▶ *You think you can fix your spouse by telling him all the things he does wrong.*

Because you cannot fix anyone but yourself, your spouse's faults are only a distraction from the real problem: You aren't meeting your own needs. Find out what they are by focusing on yourself. Then say, "I've been critical in the past because I was trying to get what I needed, but I didn't know what these needs were. Now I do. Would you be willing to listen and then help me figure out how to meet my needs?" You may be amazed at how cooperative your spouse is when you're asking for help instead of putting him down.

IT'S NEVER TOO LATE

Do you have an idea in your head that you need to have accomplished a certain amount of work by such and such a time? Or that there is a particular age at which certain things should be undertaken or learned? For example, do you believe going to school is something young people do?

Feeling too old can slow you down unnecessarily. Fear of failure or a feeling of inadequacy based on your age are attitudes that you can change. Within reason, you can do whatever you would like to do wherever you would like to do it.

YOU'VE GOT THE POWER

Change your thinking by reading the following five times a day:

"I am never too old to learn to (paint, play golf, etc.)."

"I am never too old to enjoy myself."

"I am never too old to try something new."

"I am never too old to change old habits or behaviors."

"All I need is the willingness to put into action what I desire. I want to (paint, play golf, etc.) *and I am willing to do what I need to do to achieve it.*"

☐ Break your learning down into small steps, and take them one at a time.

☐ Focus on the task at hand rather than regretting the past or worrying about the future.

☐ Keep track of your accomplishments, and congratulate yourself for every step you take.

☐ Develop your own cheering squad. Tell the friends who support you what you are doing. Have them reinforce each of the steps you take.

☐ Enjoy the *process* of what you are doing. Have fun as you keep your eye on the goal. You cannot help but become a winner.

☐ When you run up against someone who doesn't believe in you, cheerfully ignore them. Say to yourself, "If I want something I'll be able to accomplish it."

WHAT TO DO AND SAY

▶ *You always wanted to take up a hobby. Now that you have the time, you are afraid that you are too old to learn.*

When you take up a new hobby, let your teacher know you're concerned. "I feel nervous about trying this, but I'll give it my best shot."

▶ *You feel your body will not hold up under the strain of trying to get in shape.*

Check with your doctor before attempting a physical fitness program to find out if you have any limitations. Then, go for it. Tell your instructor, "I'll take things at my pace. I look forward to working with you." Don't let anyone rush you or push you beyond your comfort level.

▶ *Your boss is worried you're too old to learn a new system.*

Tell your boss, "I'm really interested in learning the new system. You know I'm a good worker, and I'll make up in effort what I initially lack in speed."

YOU *CAN* GET YOUR NEEDS MET IN A GROUP

Within a group, there is almost always one person who makes the decisions for everyone about where to go, what to do, and how to do it. If you're not that person, you may end up unhappy.

The fastest way to solve the problem is: Don't wait for anyone to ask what you think, or what you want to do, *just say it.* Speak up and make your preferences known. Be responsible for your own need for participation and power by making the moves necessary to satisfy it. The first step is to *express what that need is.*

YOU'VE GOT THE POWER

If you're not used to speaking up, tell yourself:

- ☐ "I am part of this group because I am valuable to it."

- ☐ "What I want is important enough for me to volunteer the information."

- ☐ "My opinion deserves to be heard."

- ☐ "I am willing to compromise. I may not get exactly what I asked for, but now the group is aware of what I want."

WHAT TO DO AND SAY

▶ *All of your coworkers want to go to lunch together, and you are hungry for Chinese food.*

Suggest a Chinese restaurant and ask other members of the group to support your choice. "Bill, how about Chinese for lunch?" If you're in the minority, ask, "Does anyone want to join me for Chinese food tomorrow?" Then help pick a place that has a variety of food.

▶ *You're working on a project that needs support from everyone. You have an idea that you think will work. A staff meeting has been called to discuss the project.*

Present your idea at the meeting. If your idea is turned down, but you still think it has merit, look for another area where it might fit, or another way to use it. If you have some support in the group and you're not comfortable with the final decision, don't get into a power struggle in the group. Wait until after the meeting and present your case to your boss with the others who support your position.

> ▶ *You've rented a video for the family, but your choice of movie is not popular.*

Don't take it personally. Ask, "Do you still want to watch this video?" If they say "no" or even "maybe," ask, "Are you sick of watching videos? What would you like to do instead?" If someone volunteers to get another video, let them. If you still want to see *your* video, just watch it later by yourself.

If someone is still complaining after the decision has been made, you could say, "You needed to say what you wanted when the choices were being discussed." Then let it go. Know also that there are people who are happy complaining and being miserable. Don't let yourself be made responsible for their feelings.

RELAX, YOU DON'T HAVE TO RUN EVERYTHING

We all have desires, hopes and dreams. We are taught to strive to meet the goals we set for ourselves. However, there are times when we simply can't control that process, and neither force, nor cajoling, nor manipulation, nor even effort works to guarantee we meet our goal. At these times, the wisest move may be to back off temporarily and in some cases even permanently; i.e., let it go.

The controlled letting-go of control means you consciously decide to let go of the need to run something, or to run toward something. Because you have made the choice, you are *in charge* when you purposely let go of control.

In relationships, we often try to hold onto someone we care about. But since we cannot control another person's feelings, we cannot control how the person feels about us in return. Sometimes letting go even draws that person closer because he or she feels less threatened.

Letting go facilitates living in many ways. When you are sick, you need to let go of control so you can go to bed and heal. When you make love, letting go of control allows intimacy to unfold in a trusting environment.

YOU'VE GOT THE POWER

Give yourself permission to let go of control in any situation, if you find that you need to. Define the situation carefully for yourself, being specific about the duration and circumstances in which you are willing to release control. Say it aloud, "I give myself permission to let go in this situation."

If you have a tendency to want to keep control, then slowly experiment with letting go. For example, if you schedule every hour of every day, you may want to leave two hours unscheduled during the week to see what will come up. Talk to yourself, saying soothingly,

"Take it easy." Give yourself permission to simply explore and go back to your structure if you become more anxious than you are comfortable experiencing.

Let go . . . and get on with your life.

WHAT TO DO AND SAY

▶ *You feel the flu coming on, but push yourself to stay on the job so you won't get behind in your work. You finish the project and then are off from work for a week.*

When you're getting sick, say, "I'm going to take care of myself right away so I can become more efficient again quickly. I deserve to feel good."

▶ *You spend six months trying to get a particular guy to go out with you. He doesn't return calls but you keep after him anyway, losing your self-esteem in the process.*

When someone doesn't respond to you, after a time, let the relationship go. You deserve to be with people who want to be with you. It's only a matter of choice, finding people each of us can be comfortable with. Know you are valuable and worth being around.

▶ *You keep trying to get a particular business account to sign. In the meantime, several other new accounts slip through your fingers.*

It's inefficient to keep trying to get one business account to sign when there are other opportunities available. Refusing to let go in a timely manner can cost you in the long run. Keep your end goal in sight and then pace yourself.

OTHERS RARELY WANT YOUR OPINION, JUST YOUR SUPPORT

Someone may ask you, "What do you think about this?" or "I'd like your opinion or help on this." You may think you are now safe to pass on your words of wisdom, but you may be walking into one of life's worst Catch-22s.

It is rare indeed when someone asks for your opinion and *really* wants it. Most of the time he or she is only asking for your approval. What that person really wants is to hear you say, "You're right." Even if you're absolutely certain that the other person is wrong, you may be risking irreparable damage to the relationship by saying so.

It seems silly that something as small as answering a question could cause so much trouble, but you probably already know from experience that it does. Why? Because no one in this society is supposed to need approval; everyone is supposed to be self-reliant. So they ask for approval in a backward way. Unfortunately, you end up stumbling over yourself and others don't get what they need.

YOU'VE GOT THE POWER

Be aware that some questions can be setups. A person may be stressed out and looking for an excuse to get angry with you and use your answer as a way to vent that anger. Don't let yourself be someone else's punching bag.

- ☐ Say, "Are you aware that every time you ask for my opinion, you end up angry with me? Can I help you get your feelings out in another way?"

- ☐ Then say, "I'll listen when you say, 'I'm upset,' or 'I'm hurt,' and I'll try to help you get what you need."

- ☐ If it still keeps happening, break the pattern by avoiding the setup and/or the person.

WHAT TO DO AND SAY

▶ *A friend asks you if her outfit is coordinated. It isn't.*

With questions about clothes, decide how much of a chance you are willing to take with your friend. One way to make it more palatable is to talk in terms of yourself. Instead of saying, "You should wear black shoes with that dress," you could say, "I always like to wear black shoes with that shade of blue."

If she's asking about her general appearance, find something to compliment. If you feel you are being dishonest, keep in mind that she is really asking for positive reinforcement.

▶ *Your adult child tells you about a career move he is considering.*

When an adult child or friend comes to you with a major decision he is trying to make, don't tell him your worries and don't tell him what to do. Instead, you might say, "What do *you* feel is the best thing to do?" or "What do you really want to do?" If it's obvious that he has already made the decision, then what he probably wants to hear is, "I trust your judgment" and/or "I have faith in you and know you'll succeed at whatever you decide to do."

▶   *A coworker asks what you think of a recently completed project. You think it has weaknesses.*

Unless she specifically asks for your criticisms, or unless you know her well enough to know that she wants a *really* honest answer, focus on only the positive points of the project. You don't have to lie; just find *something* to praise. Or say, "I know you can handle the project and are doing a great job."

IF YOU CAN DREAM IT, YOU CAN DO IT

If you find yourself dreaming of something, it's a good sign that it could become reality. Unless you had the innate potential for whatever you are desiring, you would not want it or especially care about it. No matter how many excuses you have learned to deny yourself your dream, it is yours for the keeping.

The exact form of the dream may vary depending on your life circumstances, but the basic desire stays the same. For example, let's suppose you dreamed of being a ballet dancer as a child but you grew too tall. If you have never been able to forget the dream, it is important that you fulfill it in some manner. Perhaps it is the movement of dance that is important to you. Or perhaps it is self-expression. In either case you can find ways to express the movement, perhaps with tai chi, dancercise, water ballet, or self-expression by orchestrating the stage movement of a play or by using your computer pen to do animation.

Your flexibility and creativity will give you the opportunity to fulfill your dreams. Use your time discovering ways to implement your dream rather than either convincing yourself why it won't work or avoiding dealing with that unfulfilled need.

Often the biggest damper to your spirits comes from people in your life who gave up their dreams and might find it too painful to see you complete yours.

YOU'VE GOT THE POWER

☐ Clearly identify your dream.

☐ Describe it in detail. Identify what it is about your dream that attracts you. What roles will it allow you to play? What do you get to do by living out this dream? (Perform, create, design, lead people, etc.) Write down your answers or tell them to another person who will be sympathetic.

☐ Identify in your mind the reasons why you can't fulfill your dream. Whose voice is stating the objections? In your mind, tell that person that you will take responsibility for your dreams and it is even okay if you don't reach it, because on the way, doors will open to you that you never knew existed.

☐ List five alternative ways to live out the characteristics of your dreams. This is like having alternative routes to get somewhere.

☐ Explore what is needed to implement each of the options that you have identified.

☐ Make plans to pursue at least one of the options right now.

☐ Keep your eye on your dream as you reach toward it, one step at a time.

☐ Be cautious about sharing your dream with others who are not supportive.

☐ Say to others who try to tell you why your dream can't work, "I'd really like you to support me on this if you can, because it's something that's important to me." If that person keeps wanting to talk about it negatively, say, "Since we have such differing opinions on this, let's talk about something else."

☐ Surround yourself with people who *will* support you.

WHAT TO DO AND SAY

▶ *You want a child but are single with no prospects for a relationship in view. You decide to adopt.*

Assuming that you have seriously examined your desire to have a child, can nurture and provide for it, seek out those agencies that arrange single-parent adoptions. If you're questioned about your plans, say, "This is just something I want for me."

▶ *You dream of owning your own business, but doubt you will be able to afford to start it up.*

Assuming you have decided the sort of business you want to run and have a viable market plan, examine your chances to get a start-up loan. Some colleges even offer courses on entrepreneurship. Gather your resources, and take it one step at a time. Be flexible in packaging your goal. Think, "*When* I get the money . . . " instead of "If . . . "

▶ *You are middle-aged, never completed college but have always wanted to be a counselor.*

The fastest-growing sector of college admissions is in older, "nontraditional" students. It is not always necessary to have a high school diploma to enroll in community college. Once you've proved to yourself that you can study as well as anyone else (older students tend to be more focused and serious about their work) then pursue the career you want.

▶ *You are pursuing your dream of being published but can't seem to get anywhere.*

When confronted with a dead end, become creative by seeking new alternatives to meet your goal. Get articles published in a company or organization newsletter, newspapers, or magazines. Write a column or try out storytelling at a library or community center. Don't listen to why you can't do something. Say to those who question you, "I'm open to any suggestions you have."

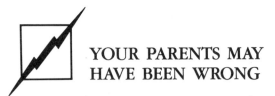

YOUR PARENTS MAY HAVE BEEN WRONG

Just because your parents told you something doesn't mean that it was true then or useful for you now. Parents usually perform only as well as they are taught, and parenting courses have only been around the last decade or so. If your parents were raised to believe that children are to be controlled and disciplined, seen and not heard, then you were probably raised that way, too. Now it may be time to ask yourself, "Is what I learned working for or against me now?"

You learned everything you needed to survive in your family, but now those lessons may be holding you back from attaining success and happiness in your personal and professional life. As a child, you had only the power your parents gave you. As an adult, you are powerful because you have choices. If you don't believe that, then you will continue to act like a child, helpless and waiting for others to make your decisions. But no one can know what will ultimately make you happy except you.

That means you need to look at all the messages you were taught and selectively choose which ones, if any, you want to keep. What's important now is not whether your parents were right or wrong, but whether the messages they gave you enable you to be the most fulfilled person you can be.

YOU'VE GOT THE POWER

Look back at your childhood and remember when your current negative behaviors began. You'll see that you were trained to be timid, insecure, self-deprecating, etc.

☐ Say to yourself: "I am not a child anymore. My world doesn't revolve around whether my parents approve of me, because I am a person with power over my own life. I trust my judgment to make the best choices for me."

☐ When you hear those old parental messages, think of yourself as a film projector or a tape recorder with a tape in it that's battered and full of flaws (negative messages).

See yourself taking out that tape and putting in a brand new one with words like, "I am a very loveable person," "I can get all of my needs met," "I have power in whatever situation I'm in," "My opinion is valuable and deserves to be heard."

You can add to that new tape whenever you want or if one of those old messages slips in, just erase it and rerecord!

WHAT TO DO AND SAY

▶ *Your parents still criticize your decisions and behavior.*

If your parents are still criticizing you and you're self-supporting, think about putting some distance between you and them until you're stronger.

If not, when your parent asks, "Why aren't you going to church, getting married, etc., like other people?" you can say, "I appreciate your concern, but I'll make my own decisions in my own time."

▶ *Your parents constantly tell you that they're unhappy because you won't do what they want.*

When your parents try to make you responsible for their feelings, say, "I don't intend to hurt you, but I can't be responsible for your feelings about what I am doing."

Say to yourself, "I may have felt I was responsible for my parents' happiness as a child, but I'm not now. I only have power and control over myself and my feelings. They'll have to take care of their own."

If your parents continue to say the same things over and over, say, "We've already discussed this before, and since we have differing views about it, I don't want to talk about it anymore. Let's talk about something else." If that doesn't work, keep the conversation short and/or just end it.

▶ *You have problems expressing your opinions.*

When you have trouble expressing your opinions, remember how your parents acted when you were a child. They may have gotten quiet, looked uncomfortable, or told you to shut up when you spoke up. Tell yourself your parents did the best they could but they were wrong. Know that what you have to say is valuable, then practice speaking up a little at a time with people who are safe and who you know will listen.

DON'T FIX—LISTEN

Except in extreme circumstances, it is important to help other people only as much as they help themselves. Doing more strips them of their power and pride.

When a person comes to you with a problem, your job is simple: listen. Unless the person specifically asks you to help, offer only a sympathetic ear. Yet many of us go into automatic pilot, starting to try to fix things whether or not we are asked to. We do this because we get uncomfortable with the other's feelings, or perhaps we like the feeling of control. Many times, fixing fends off our feelings of helplessness, so, when we try to fix things for another, we are really trying to take care of ourselves—and not the other person. We may also get involved in another's needs to distract us from taking responsibility for our own.

Listening is a communication skill. It connects two or more people, allowing each to share what is felt, thought, wanted, disliked, and needed. Listening honors the integrity of the other person. It says, "I believe you know yourself better than I, or anyone else, does. I recognize you are separate from me, and that what you say is valuable. I do not wish to dominate you but to meet you halfway in this relationship. I respect the boundaries around you that provide you with comfort."

YOU'VE GOT THE POWER

☐ Remind yourself of the value in just listening.

☐ Remind yourself that you do not know as much about the other person as that person knows.

☐ Focus your attention on the person.

☐ Realize that most people, especially when upset, do not clearly say, "Please let me blow off steam. Be on my side and don't give me any advice until I ask for it."

☐ Repeat what the other person is saying so both of you know you are hearing accurately. From time to time, nod understandingly to communicate that you understand what the person is saying.

☐ If you don't understand something say, "I don't quite understand your last remark. Can you say what you mean in another way?"

☐ Assume that your advice is not wanted unless the person specifically asks for it. Or ask, "Would you like some advice or would you rather I simply listen?"

☐ It's fine to share a story of your own but keep it short.

☐ Don't say, "I know what you feel" unless you have actually been through the situation yourself. Even then, it's better to say, "I'm sorry."

☐ If the person is talking in circles or is very disorganized, suggest a time-out. That way the person can catch his breath and collect his thoughts. Provide some nurturing, such as offering a drink of water or a reassuring smile. Slow down your own rate of talking. That will have the effect of slowing the speech of the person under stress.

☐ If the person begins to repeat herself, say, "I believe I understand your situation now. What would you like me to do?" If the person is quite upset, she may not be able to stop talking and you may need to apply the brakes by saying, "I know you're upset. We are going to stop talking about it now and go for a walk, or get a bite to eat." Use some activity to break into the conversation.

☐ If the person comes back and complains about the same thing repeatedly, you need to say, "My listening does not seem to be helping you. Perhaps you need to talk to a counselor." Then do not continue to listen.

WHAT TO DO AND SAY

▶   *A friend or coworker comes to you with a complaint about a mutual friend.*

Listen without taking sides, because you're only hearing one side of the story. Ask, "Have you talked to the person directly?" If not, encourage the person to do so. You can offer, "I will be happy to sit down with both of you to try to get things straight between you." If the person is unwilling to bring the issue up with the other person, say, "Then I can't help you." It's not up to you to run around trying to patch up half of a problem. That's a setup for failure.

▶   *Your married daughter is considering getting a divorce and wants to get your support.*

When asked for support from a child, grown or not, listen, then say, "I trust your judgment." If your daughter asks you "What do you think I should do?", say gently, "What *I* think isn't important, but I'll help you discover what you think you want to do." Then explore different options with her. "If you do _____, what do you feel will happen? What are the pros? What are the cons?" You may want to talk about practical matters. "Let's figure out your finances, child care, etc." Finally say to your daughter, "No one knows as well as you do, what is best for you. I'll support you, no matter what you decide."

LOVED ONES DON'T ALWAYS SHARE THE SAME LOVES

Just because you care for a person doesn't mean you're going to share everything in common. Your friend or partner may not want to do what you want to do, when you want to do it, and how you want to do it. Wanting to engage in a different activity does not mean that someone doesn't love you; it just means you have different interests.

There are ways for the two of you to do things together and both be happy. Instead of being disappointed in your spouse or friend because he or she doesn't share your idea of fun, find others who do. That will take the pressure off your loved one to be everything for you, and it will give the two of you more to talk about when you do spend time together.

YOU'VE GOT THE POWER

If your partner pressures you to give up an interest that he doesn't share, say, "One of the reasons I value our relationship is because we are different people."

☐ Say, "I love to share with you the things we have in common, but I need you to respect our differences."

☐ Say, "Let's talk about the ways both of us can get our needs met."

If your partner wants you to give up your friends and share hers, say, "I love you but my friends are valuable to me, too. I accept your friends and I need you to accept mine."

If the problem persists, your partner may be harboring insecurities left over from childhood, and you might want to consult a marriage counselor.

WHAT TO DO AND SAY

▶ *You make plans to do something you enjoy, and then your partner says he won't go.*

When you want to do something together but you haven't asked your partner, have an alternative ready in case he says he has other plans or that he just doesn't want to go. That way, you won't feel that he is keeping you from doing what you want because it's not something he wants. You can offer the alternative to him but present it without any expectations or pressure.

▶ *You are excited about an invitation to a party, but your spouse is concerned about getting bored there.*

If your spouse is interested in going with you but concerned that he'll end up being bored, take two cars, or make plans for one of you to get a ride home with another guest so the other can leave. Your loved one will be happy to be with you because he isn't doing something he was forced into, and he'll have an out if he decides he's not comfortable.

▶ *One spouse likes to go to family gatherings and the other doesn't.*

If you're the spouse who doesn't like to go to family gatherings because you're uncomfortable with some of the members, either find someone there you do like and spend the time with her, or don't go that often. If you're the spouse who does like family get-togethers, go to some of them by yourself. The family might enjoy seeing you alone!

WHAT YOU ADMIRE IN OTHERS YOU ALREADY HAVE IN YOURSELF

Whenever you see attributes in another person that you admire, you are actually getting a preview of coming attractions within your own self. You would not be attracted to those characteristics if you did not already have the potential to develop them. It is the familiarity and fit that catches your attention.

Part of the attraction comes because it seems as if the other person has "it" and you don't. But what you're feeling is only the difference between actuality and potential. Your time will come if you simply work to develop the trait. Of course, this part is up to you. No one can develop it for you, but no one can keep you from it either. Rejoice when you are attracted to someone else's attributes. Appreciate them. Claim them for yourself.

YOU'VE GOT THE POWER

- ☐ Realize that what you admire is already a part of you.

- ☐ Examine the dimensions of the trait in the other person. What is it about the trait that captures your attention?

- ☐ Figure out how to develop this same trait in yourself. It may take some time, but rest assured you will realize you are looking at your future if you will just let yourself develop.

- ☐ Say to yourself, "I have this potential within me. I am becoming more _____ day by day."

- ☐ If you find this hard to believe, ask yourself what you were taught that blocked the possibility in your mind of having this trait. Who or what told you that you weren't, for example, "creative." Then, in your imagination, say, "I give myself permission to have any characteristics that I'm attracted to."

WHAT TO DO AND SAY

▶ *You wish you were creative like the painter down the street.*

Your creativity may take the form of painting or express itself in other ways. You may shine at a certain craft or be a wonderful interior decorator. Once you've found the area to express your talent, enjoy the actuality. Say, "I am creative. I release the blocks to my dreams. I will persevere."

▶ *You wish you were as outgoing as your friend.*

Notice how your friend acts around other people. She smiles a lot, listens well, remembers birthdays, and makes considerate gestures. You start experimenting on your own.

▶ *You admire the work of the technical designer in your company. Your mind spins wonderful projects that you don't have the skill to create.*

When you are attracted to an area of expression that requires technical skill, it's a good idea to begin learning some of those skills. When you acquire facility in those areas, it's only a matter of time until you can create your own projects. Or, you may want to collaborate with someone who has the skills you lack.

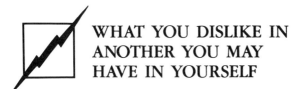

WHAT YOU DISLIKE IN ANOTHER YOU MAY HAVE IN YOURSELF

If you find yourself angry or upset with a characteristic in another person, it may be that you have the same characteristic in yourself but are disowning it. Psychologically, you give that person responsibility for *your* trait. The intensity of your feeling of anger, resentment, unbending judgment, or stark criticism lets you know what you are doing. Rather than experience the pain of feeling something within ourselves that we don't like, we project the feelings onto another person.

By becoming aware of what bothers us in others, we have a golden opportunity to learn about ourselves and fix what makes us uncomfortable. That way we take the power to change for the better.

YOU'VE GOT THE POWER

☐ Pay attention to feelings of dislike, hate, resentment, or disgust about others.

☐ Realize you have an opportunity to learn more about yourself.

☐ Study the person whom you feel so strongly about.

☐ Look within yourself for a similar trait. You may benefit from asking the question, "What is it within me that is being triggered?" or "When did I experience a situation that caused a similar feeling in me?"

☐ Become silent and wait for an answer. You will hear, see, or feel something within your mind that recalls a situation from your own life.

☐ Talk to the child within you saying, "It's okay now. I accept you as you are."

☐ Restructure the scene in your mind so that the next time the scene can have a different outcome—one that you like.

WHAT TO DO AND SAY

▶ *A critical colleague scolds your friend and you become irate. You feel like you are being punched in the stomach.*

If you are sensitive to criticism, you are likely to be very self critical. Thank your critical part because it has been serving a purpose. It has helped you feel more in control of getting what you want, such as approval from those you depend upon.

Tell yourself that you are responsible and can relax. Give yourself permission to let go of your critical part. Be a friend to yourself, not a judge.

Look at the offending person who started this whole thing and mentally thank that person for acting as a trigger for the chance to improve yourself. Then detach yourself emotionally from the incident.

▶ *You see people marching for a cause shouting venomous slogans at those with whom they disagree. There is no willingness to negotiate differences.*

Activists almost always have a hidden psychological agenda: a part of themselves that feels better when they are fighting for a cause. They are simultaneously fighting for a part of themselves. If you meet with one personally, there is no point in engaging in an argument. Rather, say, "I realize you feel strongly about this. I feel differently. I'd be willing to try to understand what you feel . . . not what you think."

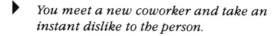 *You meet a new coworker and take an instant dislike to the person.*

Say, "I know we haven't spent a lot of time together. I'd like to get to know you better. Would you like to go out to lunch?" Then, look for aspects in yourself that are reflected in that person. Maybe you will understand both yourself and your coworker better.

WE'RE ALL ALIKE IN THAT WE'RE DIFFERENT

There are books, magazine articles, and studies aplenty that talk about the differences in people: the psychological differences between men and women, the cultural differences between East and West, the religious differences between societies and sects.

What you have in common with other people is that each one of you is different. Whatever group a person belongs to, he or she is still an individual, separate and unique.

YOU'VE GOT THE POWER

Because we know ourselves best, it is sometimes easy to assume that everyone else thinks the same way we do.

□ Tell yourself, "The only person I really know is me. I do not know what anyone else is really thinking or feeling unless I ask."

In your transactions with others, ask "What do you think about _____?" or "How do you feel about _____?" Then give them the opportunity to explain.

WHAT TO DO AND SAY

▶ *Your twelve-year-old son's room is in constant chaos. You can't understand why he can't keep it tidy.*

State your own feelings or thoughts first. Don't accuse. Say, "I'm upset because I don't understand why you can't keep your room clean. Can we talk about it?"

Your child may say the room is his private space and it's fine the way it is. You can accept that or say, "I'm not comfortable. Can we discuss some alternatives?"

What's important is that you don't expect him to

automatically adopt your way. Focus on how you can possibly change your attitude. For instance you may agree to the room being a private space and you won't enter without first knocking. Your child may agree to remove all the dirty laundry. This might be a good opportunity to practice the fine art of reaching a compromise.

▶ *You are around people of different back-grounds and can't seem to get along with any of them.*

Check out your attitude and see if you haven't learned prejudices that are standing in your way. Knowledge is always the surest way to bridge differences. Also, some cultures discourage talking about thoughts and feelings openly. If so, you may want to do a little investigation into their belief systems so that you can understand more and come up with a comfortable form of communication.

▶ *You can't understand what your daughter sees in her new boyfriend.*

When your children start building relationships of their own, they have to be allowed their choices. If the relationship is truly unsuitable, it will probably end at some point (hopefully before they get married). By criticizing your daughter's choice of boyfriend, you risk drawing her closer to him as a point of rebellion. Instead, say, "I'd really like to get to know your friend," and include him in a family event or ask him to dinner.

BE PROTECTIVE:
THERE REALLY ARE
BAD GUYS OUT THERE

There really *are* bad guys out there. Not everyone is as nice as you, as honest or trustworthy. Actually they are not "bad" people, but rather they are out of control with their feelings. Because they will do anything to get what they want they have the ability to hurt you.

They cannot help themselves. Early on in their lives, they could not trust the people who took care of them to meet their needs. Because their needs weren't met, and they didn't have adequate role models, they didn't learn to feel empathy for others.

Empathy is the feeling that allows us to feel *with* another person; i.e., feel what they feel. That is why most of us don't want to hurt another person because we know what it's like to be hurt and we would feel their hurt. Without empathy, no morals, no self-control, and no conscience can develop.

It is sad, indeed, that bad guys exist. Your job is to see that you do not fall victim to one.

To be conned, you must want something for nothing, be vulnerable, or simply be unaware of the danger. Failure to check into a person's background or the history of a project can lead to being taken. Also, listening to only what a person says, instead of watching the behavior and making sure the words match the behavior, leads to victimization.

YOU'VE GOT THE POWER

Don't assume that everyone who is nice to you automatically has your best interests at heart.

- ☐ *Never* pay to have your emotional needs met.

- ☐ Don't assume that someone who is nice to you has your best interests at heart.

- ☐ Make sure that a person's words match their behavior.

- ☐ If something sounds too good to be true—it probably is.

WHAT TO DO AND SAY

▶   *You are lonely and single. An attractive man down on his luck romances you, promising to buy you many lovely things as soon as his "deal" comes through. Meanwhile, you pay for everything you two do together.*

When someone preys on your loneliness, realize that letting yourself be used is a short-term cure that saps you of your self-esteem. Be firm and end the relationship by saying "I don't believe in you anymore. I'm going to move on with my life without you." Then make friends who accept you freely.

▶   *You answer the doorbell and discover an eager student selling magazines for a good cause.*

When the proverbial salesperson tries to sell you something you may not need, say, "I'm glad you are so enthusiastic, but I do not need ten subscriptions. I'll buy one." If the salesperson continues to persist, say, "If you persist, I can't even buy one." DO NOT take responsibility for the other person's goals. Take only what is beneficial to you and no more.

▶   *A deal is offered to you that sounds too good to be true.*

Do not be hurried. Check the deal out in a businesslike manner. Ask yourself, "If it's so good why are there still opportunities?" Be suspicious. Though your pathway to success may take longer, you may be just as satisfied with following it.

MORE THINGS DON'T ALWAYS MEAN MORE HAPPINESS

Every time we turn on the TV or the radio or pick up a newspaper or magazine, we're bombarded with advertising that says, "The more you have, the happier you'll be! Use our product and you will be more popular/loveable/successful!" Remember, this is only an advertiser's technique to make you feel that something is missing from your life because you don't have their product. Truthfully, happiness still comes from within. Material possessions are merely icing on the cake.

Your attitude towards those possessions is important. Use them as tools to make your life more pleasant, but more important is the knowledge that you can be happy without all the toys.

Remember: you are a worthwhile person simply because you exist. Your value to the world lies in your ability to give rather than receive. Give the positive energy that comes from looking for joy in whatever you're doing instead of worrying about the quantity of your things.

There is also a great price to be paid for the accumulation of stuff. It takes time to make money and to maintain all your possessions. A luxury sports car is great but it's difficult to find a good mechanic and extremely costly to have it repaired.

Worse is the loss of peace of mind, relationships, and intimacy with family and friends as you spend your time making more money to buy more things. You may even lose valuable parts of yourself in the process because you don't have the time to cultivate them.

WHAT TO DO AND SAY

▶ *Your coworkers are always bragging around the coffee machine about their latest acquisitions.*

When your coworkers brag about their new toys, it does not mean that they are better than you. They are making statements about their lack of self-worth and their belief that their things are the most important part of them. Don't buy into their insecurity by trying to compete with them.

Tell yourself you're valuable, naked, and penniless, and whatever you need, you will work towards acquiring. Without the responsibility of things you don't really need, you will have more freedom, and time to devote to loved ones and yourself.

Tell the braggarts: "I'm happy for you" or "That's great." It's okay to change the subject if you've heard enough. Then look for friends and colleagues who value people more than possessions.

▶ *You feel sad when you can't afford to buy new things.*

If you feel sad over what you can't afford, ask yourself "Why?" If the sadness has to do with your lack of money, find other ways to make yourself happy, like going to the park, reading a good book, or volunteering your time and making someone else smile.

If, however, your sadness is a distraction from an emotional problem that has nothing to do with buying things, consider counseling.

▶ *You envy others the same age or younger than you who have more than you.*

With someone who's your age or younger and more successful, remind yourself that people move at their own pace. Say, "I will have what I want. It's only a matter of time." Remember that your goals are different from anyone else's because of your individuality. Keep your focus on how happy you are making yourself and other people's success won't be that important.

WATCH YOUR BOUNDARIES

There are two kinds of boundaries that affect each of us. One is the physical space that we keep around ourselves that allows us to be comfortable; the other might be termed psychological space. If you *feel* someone has come physically too close to you, even if that person doesn't touch you, or if someone's physical touch feels uncomfortable, then they have undoubtedly crossed into your physical space. Someone crosses into your psychological space when he or she tries to tell you what to do, how to do it, and generally tries to run your life. Another type of boundary crosser tells you how you feel or how you *should* feel. No one can tell you these things. Only you know what you feel and what you want to do.

You have a right to be your own protector, and you must, in fact, take responsibility for the job. No one but you knows for sure where your boundaries lie.

YOU'VE GOT THE POWER

Some people like physical closeness and enjoy being hugged. Others want two or three feet between themselves and others until they get to know the other person well. If someone comes closer to you than you are comfortable with, simply back away. If the person insists on touching your arm or shoulder, say "I realize you are only trying to be friendly, but I'd feel more comfortable if you didn't touch me."

WHAT TO DO AND SAY

▶   *You admit to yourself that you have been the victim of incest.*

As a child you were unable to protect yourself from intrusion, and because of that you must not feel guilty about what occurred. But it will probably take professional help to assist you in getting over the effects. Seek that help when *you* are ready. Above all, realize that no one has the right to cross your boundaries, and as an adult it is up to you to take responsibility for protecting yourself from intrusion.

▶   *Another person states that you will like dia-monds, the mountain resort, or whatever, without asking whether you do like it.*

If someone tries to tell you how or what to feel, say, "I realize *you* like diamonds (or mountain resorts) but I don't." Even close friends or family can assume, erroneously, that they know how you feel. It's up to you to set them straight, gently but firmly.

▶   *Your dinner date insists on ordering for you. You're getting over the flu and all you really want is a light meal.*

Ask the waiter to give you a few minutes. Then explain to your date that you prefer to order for yourself. If he persists with, "You'll *love* the cod provençal—it's the house specialty," hold your ground and say, "No, *you* will love the cod provençal—I'd like consommé and a small salad."

YOU DON'T HAVE TO BE RIGHT ALL THE TIME

Intolerance means a lack of willingness to acknowledge other people's beliefs. It demands that others believe and act as you do. And it requires that you are always seen as right and others as wrong. But being right rarely means you will be truly happy. If your goal is to get along with people, intolerance will widen the gap between you and others instead of bridging it.

The key to getting along with other people is flexibility. Know that what you believe is right for you. It may be right for others but it isn't your job to convince them. Even those who think similarly won't agree with you on everything. So find grounds of commonality and concentrate on those rather than on the differences.

YOU'VE GOT THE POWER

When you feel the urge to be "right" coming on, stop and ask yourself, "Is it really worth it to have the last word in this situation?" If you feel that it will put a stop to your communication with that person, it's probably not.

If someone is earnestly trying to prove to you how "right" they are, smile and say, "What works for you may not work equally well for me." Then change the subject.

WHAT TO DO AND SAY

▶   *You and your neighbor can't be friends because you're always arguing over political issues.*

Try to find out your neighbor's interests besides potentially "hot" issues like religion and politics. You could share a love of family, friends, exercise, food, movies, sports, music, and books. It's okay to just avoid the subjects you can't agree on.

With political fights, say, "That's an interesting point," and then change the subject. Don't let yourself be dragged into an argument you don't want to be a part of.

▶   *You and your spouse argue over who's right instead of getting your needs met.*

If you and your spouse are stuck in proving who's right, someone is probably feeling powerless to get what they want and covering it up. Sit down with your spouse and say, "I don't want to be right anymore. I want to find out what both of our needs are and how we can help each other meet them."

▶ *You volunteer with a person of a different religion who's constantly trying to convert you.*

With proselytizers, say, "I'm comfortable with my spiritual beliefs as they are," or "I don't want to talk about religion but I'd like to chat with you about other things like _____," and focus on what you do want to discuss. If they keep pressing, say, "I respect your right to your beliefs and I need you to respect my right to mine. I don't want to talk about this anymore."

▶ *Your coworker is from another culture and doesn't accept your differences.*

If a colleague's lack of acceptance just keeps him from being very social, then you may want to ignore his attitude and keep doing a good job. If you are confronted, or his beliefs are preventing the work from being done, then you could say, "I understand you have a bias but it's important that we focus on the job at hand."

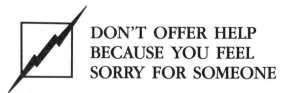

DON'T OFFER HELP BECAUSE YOU FEEL SORRY FOR SOMEONE

Fixing someone else's life because you feel sorry for that person interferes with that person's sense of being valuable. It is one thing to do for those less capable what they cannot do for themselves. It is quite another to feel sorry for a person and to communicate "You poor thing." That carries a judgment with it.

Your feeling of pity adds emotion to the mix. It adds a judgment or evaluation to the situation. Emotions also obscure thinking and planning. With compromised faculties, you won't be as able to see what is really necessary to improve the situation. So, both of you lose. The person being helped is made to feel inadequate. The one helping is likely to get tired of helping and pull away.

Whatever you do or say because you feel sorry for someone tends to be directed to helping that person feel better rather than being of assistance to their situation. Although you may help someone feel better temporarily, the person eventually has to face the music. It is not unusual for the one helped to become angry at the fixer at a later time.

YOU'VE GOT THE POWER

Recognize that your emotion of feeling sorry belongs to *you*. It has nothing to do with the situation and is not likely to be a clear reflection of what the other person genuinely needs.

☐   Help the person understand how he or she got into the situation by analyzing the problem.

☐   Help the person with long-term planning.

☐   Say, "I'm sorry you are having trouble. Would you like me to try to help you figure out what is wrong so you can fix it?"

☐ When you feel sorry for someone with money problems, remember that giving someone money simply puts off the inevitable. It enables a person to stay helpless.

WHAT TO DO AND SAY

▶ *Your recently divorced friend can't make her house payment and you are tempted to offer money.*

Be a companion to your grieving friend. Say, "I'm sorry you are losing your house. Let's talk about how you can get your feet on the ground and eventually get a new house."

▶ *Your coworker is always falling behind in collecting receivables and you want to stay late and help her.*

Often we remember how painful it was for us when we were in a similar situation. You may be offering to do your coworker's job to relieve your own painful memory. The trouble is, your friend still doesn't know how to efficiently do the job. Instead, sit down with your friend and act as a coach. Say, "I remember how hard it was when I was first learning, but you'll get there. Here are some ideas that helped me." Then offer some tips. Finish by saying, "You'll learn. I have confidence in you."

▶ *Your eight-year-old is rejected by his friends and you wonder if you should try to fix the*

*situation yourself, maybe by buying him a
new and popular toy.*

When you feel sorry for your child and try to fix the
hurt feelings, the cause of the problem goes un-
treated. Instead, it's imperative to discover *why* the
child is having problems. Observe the youngster
around other kids and talk to teachers, coaches, and
other parents. Don't hesitate to seek the aid of a counselor. Be straight with your child, saying, "You're a
super person. There is some reason other kids don't
recognize it. A counselor will help us figure out this
problem and we'll fix it so you can *have* friends and *be*
a good friend."

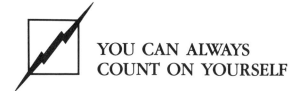

YOU CAN ALWAYS
COUNT ON YOURSELF

You may have found yourself disappointed or let
down because the people you cared about weren't
there when you needed them. But the most important person is always there for you, and that's yourself. You can always depend on yourself in the worst
and best of times. Be your own best friend with
words of encouragement and love. No one else can
promise to help you with every choice you make and
stay with you always.

We all have a need to feel safe. The need may stem
from the time when we were infants and totally protected, and continues because the world is a scary

place. What's vital to know is that none of us wants to feel abandoned.

So we control and manipulate the people and events around us, precariously balancing them all until—bang—the next problem hits! Then we're looking for someone or something to give us the answers that will keep us from feeling helpless and alone.

We rush off to doctors, counselors, psychics, bartenders, and best friends searching for the secret to our pain. True, they can offer support and advice when you're facing a problem. But there's a difference between asking input on your alternatives and desperately seeking relief.

Look for reassurance within yourself, because you are the one person who is always there to give it.

YOU'VE GOT THE POWER

Before you turn to a friend with a problem, stop and ask yourself, "Is this a problem that I really need advice about or am I just scared?" You'll know you're scared if there's an ache in your stomach that's beyond the confusion in your head. The way to get past your fear is:

☐ Take a few moments and visualize yourself in your favorite place.

☐ See yourself as two people with one of you comforting the other. Sit in front of a mirror and talk to your image as if it's another person. Say, "You can count on me."

☐ Tell that image, "I love you and only want the best for you. I will always try to help you make the best decisions for your life, but most importantly, I will never leave you. Whatever changes occur in your life I will always be there for you."

You'll find yourself meeting your problems with the firm self-assurance of one who knows that she is truly safe.

WHAT TO DO AND SAY

▶ *You call a friend every time a crisis comes up.*

Before you make that phone call, pause and give yourself the chance to think. Ask yourself, "Is this crisis really a matter of life and death?" Realize that if the answer were "yes," you'd be calling 911.

Take a deep breath and ask yourself, "Why do I always call on my friend to solve my problems?" Hold a dialogue with yourself. Say, "I always call my friend because _____."

Then ask yourself what you think your friend will say to you about *this* problem. Give the answer: I think my friend will say _____."

Think about the answer. Congratulate yourself for not making the phone call. Give yourself permission to feel secure: You've just discovered a new friend—yourself.

▶ *You're getting plenty of advice and support from others but you're still worried.*

If you are getting plenty of advice and support but are still worried about a problem, it may be because you've got so much advice that it is confusing and contradictory.

Take a piece of paper and write your problem at the top of it. List all of the advice you've received in one column, including any options you thought of yourself. In the second column, write the words "yes" or "no," depending on whether you think each option is helpful. Then cross out all of the "no's."

Use what's left to help you create your own solution.

Give yourself permission to feel more secure because you've taken steps to end some of your confusion.

LISTEN TO YOUR BODY

Most of us subscribe to that wonderful Puritan worn ethic that says you must do more than anyone else or you're not trying, and you're not really successful. Sad, isn't it? But the real truth is, no matter how much you try to convince your body otherwise, there are more than twenty-four hours in a day, that you don't need rest and relaxation, your body will fight to prove you wrong.

Our bodies generally know what is best for us. To ignore what feels good or bad is asking for trouble.

Sooner or later, ignoring our bodies catches up with us, raising the likelihood of accidents and illness.

Pacing is crucial: some work, some play, and some rest. A varied schedule works best for most people.

Fatigue is a killer. It makes the whole world look much worse than it is. It makes us vulnerable to what others say as well as to their actions. It numbs our faculties, making it hard for us to reason well. Often, after a good rest, the problems we do have seem more manageable. For one thing, we have a better ability to think them through and come to some rational solution.

Overlooking the needs of your body lowers efficiency. You won't be as proficient and you'll make mistakes.

YOU'VE GOT THE POWER

Don't wait until your body breaks down. When you feel tired, rest in whatever way fits you. For some it will be a ten-minute nap. For others, a "Mental Health" day will do the trick. Be certain to rest before you attempt to solve any major problem. You may then discover that you don't have a problem after all. Even if you do, you'll have an easier time finding a viable solution.

- ☐ Delegate what tasks you can, across the board, at work and at home.

- ☐ Talk to yourself, giving the worker part of you permission to ease up.

- ☐ Give yourself permission to play. Then make time to do it. Let yourself put off until tomorrow the last half of a task. And, by all means, let the lawn grow for another day or even week, while you take care of yourself.

WHAT TO DO AND SAY

▶   *You're doing what you love, but you are still burning out.*

Take a "Mental Health" day whenever you can, where you do something just for yourself. *Don't* use it to "catch up" on anything you're behind in—it will get done, eventually. Get as far away from work as you can. At work, take some breaks where you can do some deep breathing exercises.

▶   *You notice yourself yelling more at the kids after you have pushed yourself to make things* just right *for them.*

When you yell at the kids, apologize and then say, "I'm going to take a rest. You handle dinner and the laundry." It may not be great but they'll survive and be grateful for a rested parent. You may even find they'll *send* you to bed the next time you start yelling. If it's the yelling of others that's setting you off, stop whatever you're doing. Say, "Hang on a minute." Take a deep breath, clear your head, and begin again.

▶   *You have had nagging tiredness and keep getting colds. You skipped your vacation this year.*

Arrange to take some time off. If that is not possible, get extra rest and put time into building yourself up. It takes awhile to recuperate from neglect. Give yourself what you need. It's smart in the long run.

PASS ON THE HELP YOU'VE RECEIVED TO SOMEONE ELSE

If you're willing to accept it, there will always be people who want to help you. Some of them will know what you want of them without your even asking. You may be able to pay them back directly with a favor. But there are lots of people that you can't do anything for who will still lend you a hand.

You still may feel very grateful for the help you've received, but you can't pay it back directly either because the person doesn't want it, they're not available, or they don't need it. A perfect way to express that gratitude is to help someone who can't do anything for you.

When you help someone else, instead of demanding something directly in return, give yourself freely in the name of those who didn't demand a price from you.

But whenever you help anyone for any reason, you automatically set yourself up for the favor to be returned, because the person you helped will be looking for an opportunity to repay what they were given. If you can't think of any favor you want in return, suggest that they do a favor for someone else. Letting go of anything opens up room for more to come into your life and the lives of others.

YOU'VE GOT THE POWER

Tell yourself that helpful people do exist and that you will find them.

- ☐ Say "thank you" for any help and send a handwritten note or card.

- ☐ Look for opportunities to help others. It will keep your own situation in perspective.

- ☐ Pass on that help even if it isn't anything more than telling someone that she's doing a great job!

WHAT TO DO AND SAY

▶ *You need advice about what to do about a problem.*

For advice, think of someone you admire and say, "I know we don't know each other that well but I respect your opinion a great deal and wondered if you had some advice for me about _____?" Most people love to be asked for their thoughts.

▶ *You want to help someone just starting out in the world as you were helped ten years ago.*

Look for enthusiastic and smart workers who could use your support. You may be able to offer help directly with advice or contacts. Or you could work behind the scenes, recommending them to people you know who are looking for professionals with lots of potential.

▶   *You need a loan from a family member to get through the next few months.*

Money is a very touchy issue. If you need to borrow, ask for the money, state the reasons why, and tell how you plan to pay it back. If you can't live up to the arrangement later, tell the person and give what you can. Don't avoid it and hope it will go away. Be honest, because it's what you'll want when you give to someone else down the road.

DON'T DO THINGS BECAUSE YOU'RE AFRAID

It's unwise to make decisions or take action when we are afraid, because fear indicates something is wrong with the situation we are in. When you feel afraid, you may not have access to all the information you need to make a wise decision. Or, you may be trying to do what you *should* do, not what you want to do. You may be trying to do something that doesn't fit you or isn't right for you. In these cases, your fears are acting as a protection for you.

Another kind of protection occurs when we have old emotional business to take care of. An example of this is the fear that sweeps over a person who was sexually abused as a child when he or she is faced with adult sexual intimacy. That person needs to heal the child within who experienced abuse before entering a sexually demanding environment as an adult. It is good that the fear is there to highlight the need.

Sometimes we are afraid to do something because we need to gain more skills before tackling the job. Fear keeps us from getting in over our heads. That is a legitimate fear which is easily remedied if recognized.

When you are afraid *not* to do something for another person, you are selling yourself short. Fears of abandonment and rejection make you especially vulnerable to feeling that you "have" to do things that you would not ordinarily do.

Fear also obscures our ability to think clearly, to make rational decisions, and to act wisely. With our minds clouded by fear, we are likely to get into more trouble than we would if we didn't act at all.

What we're *not* talking about:

1. Mild fleeting apprehension in a new situation. (But even here, take a deep breath before proceeding.)

2. Constant worriers who need the help of a professional.

YOU'VE GOT THE POWER

☐ Your main goal is to discover the source of your fear and then fix it. At that point, decisions and action will become simple. Say to yourself, "There's a reason I'm afraid." Then ask your inner guidance system what it is. An answer will come.

☐ Do not hesitate to be honest and ask for more time when you are feeling indecisive. Say, "I need to sort through my feelings about the issues before I give an answer," or "I need to think through what I really want to do before I give you an answer." Buy time.

WHAT TO DO AND SAY

▶ *As you plan for your wedding, you become fearful that you've made the wrong choice in a spouse. You begin to think you probably have.*

Reassess your feelings. Look deep within yourself to determine what you're feeling and why. You *must* be honest with yourself. Ask yourself whether you are afraid you'll never be married unless you marry this person who is available now. Or perhaps you are afraid your parents will get mad at you because the wedding invitations are already printed. If you decide that you are not ready to marry, say to your parents, "I'm sorry for the inconvenience but I'm not ready to get married. I'll help with clearing things up." To your fiancé, "I'm sorry, I'm simply not ready to marry you now and it would be misleading to do what doesn't feel right to me."

▶ *You're afraid to go to your boss to ask for a raise. You probably either sense: 1) It's a bad time to approach the boss, or 2) You need more information or preparation before you can be effective.*

Address your boss *after* you have thought through what you want and why you want it. Do your home-work. Be flexible about when you ask to see your boss. Make sure it's a convenient time and say, "I appreciate your giving me this time." Then, briefly, lay out your job history with the company, outline your contributions, your business objectives, and why you are a valuable employee. Finally, say, "I feel I am worth _____ to the company," quoting the figure you wish to receive. Whether you get the raise or not, you should be proud of the way you handled the situation.

▶   *You engage in sexual relations when you don't feel like it because you are afraid your partner will leave you if you don't. And you're afraid to be alone.*

Work on your ability to be alone with yourself. Then say to the person, "I love you, but I don't want sex now." If the person rejects you, say, "You do what you need to do to take care of yourself. I'm okay being true to myself." Then realize you are better off with-out that individual.

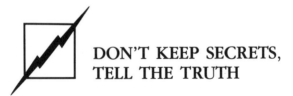

DON'T KEEP SECRETS, TELL THE TRUTH

Withholding information that affects another person always has an impact on that person. Even though you think you're protecting someone, he or she may be more hurt by not knowing than knowing. Unlike confidentiality, where you both mutually agree to keep the information private, such an agreement is not struck when secrets are abroad.

A common example is the adopted child who does not know of the adoption. A well-intentioned family fears their child will be hurt if he knows he is adopted, so they don't tell him. The parents think the knowledge is buried and that everyone is safe from the pain of the truth.

The fact is, almost everyone is hurt by the repercussions of the secret being kept, especially the person who is supposedly protected. The parents will always have the truth in the back of their minds and will be constantly on guard, ready to change what they say and do in order to keep the secret. The child will likely sense all of this and may think it's because there is something wrong with him.

The facts often don't match the story that is given, because there is a piece missing. It's not uncommon for the person to put everything together and come to the same conclusion that would have been reached had the truth been known.

In addition, the person may feel betrayed because he was lied to, but still not be able to confront the holders of the secret for fear that he will now hurt them. So the cycle may continue with everyone losing out.

When a secret is held, it may not have been intentional. Perhaps the right moment to communicate it was just missed. Or it just happened. But once it did, it's not unusual to feel helpless about how to get out of the situation. When the truth is known, the person may think, "If that was kept secret, then what else has been kept secret?" But she may also be greatly relieved because the information may confirm what she has been thinking and feeling all along.

Secrets always cause trouble and the consequences of keeping them do not get any better after any amount of time.

YOU'VE GOT THE POWER

When you have information that affects another person, ask yourself, "What effect is there likely to be on that person?"

☐ If you notice a conflict of interest, say so to the person confiding in you, "I'm beginning to feel uncomfortable. Stop giving me any more information until we decide whether it's a good idea for you to continue or not."

☐ Then be completely honest about whether you want to know. Say, "This information puts me in the middle. I don't want to hear any more."

WHAT TO DO AND SAY

▶   *Your best buddy at work is planning a career change and tells you in confidence.*

When your buddy tells you about a career change, you may instantly know where your loyalties lie and can keep his confidence totally. If, however, his move could cost your company a lot of money, say to your buddy, "I'm concerned about what you're telling me." Say why and ask him to take responsibility for the information and/or solve the problem. Tell him not to tell you anything else until you know his plan.

▶   *You are asked by your best friend whether her husband is having an affair. You know the answer because you saw him romantically kissing another woman in a restaurant.*

When your best friend asks about her husband's extracurricular love life, you are on the spot. Ask her what she suspects and encourage her to trust her feelings and confront her husband. Don't get caught in the middle or be tempted to tell what you know. It is your friend's problem and she has to handle it.

▶   *Large layoffs and personnel changes are forthcoming in the corporation where you are a mid-manager, but upper management decided to keep them a secret to avoid disruption to production. Unfortunately, the scheme is backfiring with productivity plunging to an all-time low.*

If you know about a future personnel move at work and are confronted by an employee who will be affected, simply say: "I'm sorry that I cannot answer you now. I will let you know as soon as I can." Do not lie. Point out that you cannot abandon your responsibility to your company. It's a fact of the business world.

As an employee, realize that all business secrets are not necessarily bad. If you sense a secret brewing, continue to do your job well, but be prepared for change. Assure yourself that you can adapt.

FRIENDS SERVE MANY PURPOSES

Friends come in all sizes, shapes, and interests. One friend may be a sports buddy, another a confidant. Sometimes friends will fill more than one need in your life, but seldom does one friend serve all your needs. Trying to make a friend be more than what he or she is comfortable being is sure to lead to stress.

YOU'VE GOT THE POWER

When a friend cannot give you what you feel you need at the moment, take that person for what she realistically can offer and let go of the rest.

The reverse is also true. If you find that a friend whose company you enjoy is backing away from you, it does not necessarily mean that you are in any way inadequate. Your friend may not turn to you in a time of need because doing so may not be part of your relationship.

WHAT TO DO AND SAY

▶ *Your golf partner backs away when you start to talk about your marriage or your feelings.*

With your golf partner, realize that she may enjoy the weekly game as a recreational break, and thus be uncomfortable with sharing private feelings. If you can't concentrate so lightheartedly on the game now, tell your friend you are having some problems that interfere with your enjoyment of the game, but will play as soon as you have sorted them out. You might want to add how much you are looking forward to that time.

▶ *You want to socialize with a close working buddy but he is busy, so you suggest break-fast. He says, "Sometime! We'll get together, sometime!" You feel put off and don't understand because you work so well together.*

Many people like to keep their working and their personal lives separate. Their reasons may have more to do with them than you. Be kind and don't push your colleague. Allow him his privacy. Simply accept the person as is, enjoy what is offered and stop trying to get more.

▶ *You and your friend have never talked about personal matters, but you found out there are problems at home. You're not sure whether to bring it up.*

When you know your friend is going through problems, you can say, "I know we've never gotten into personal issues but I want you to know that I am available as a listener if you would like to talk to me." Then, back off.

FRIENDSHIPS TAKE TIME

Friends can play a vital part in your support, learning, and fun. But the important thing to remember is that friendships take time. You may meet some people and feel you've known them all your life when it's only been ten minutes. Others you may feel close to because you work together or belong to the same group. Still others may look like prime candidates for buddies because they live close to you.

No matter what your feelings are, it will take time, experiences, and even a few falling-outs before you develop a true friendship. Each person has varying requirements, expectations, and perceptions of what friendship is. Those will be defined and refined as you travel down the same road together. You may think that the person has certain characteristics but you'll discover if your first impressions were right or wrong only with the passage of time.

Shared experiences and shared feelings are what make up a friendship. They can tell you the value of a relationship and whether it's a developing or short-term one.

YOU'VE GOT THE POWER

Know that your friends are not responsible for your happiness—you are. So keep taking care of your own needs.

☐ Decide what qualities you want in your friends.

☐ Be willing to let time reveal those qualities rather than make quick judgments. Just because you have warm feelings for people or like them immediately does not make them 100 percent trustworthy. You'll only discern that as you work out situations together.

☐ Remember that people can only be what they are capable of being. They may not have intended to let you down, or they may simply be unable to live up to your expectations. They were just being themselves.

☐ Be honest with yourself and don't try to change them. If they don't have the characteristics you want in a friend, let them go. If they do but in a way different from what you'd like, decide if you can accept their quirks and style.

WHAT TO DO AND SAY

▶ *Friends have treated you poorly in the past and you don't want it to happen again.*

If your former friends treated you badly, you probably made poor choices. Now that you know what you want, trust your judgment in finding new people. No one wants to be interrogated about their potential as a friend, however, so go slowly, watch and listen, but do so casually. When you see some quality you like, reinforce it by saying, "I really appreciate _____ about you," or "You have an interesting way of saying things—I like it."

Be cautious, but don't let yourself be a victim of skepticism because the person might sense it and begin to avoid you. With practice, you'll find the right balance.

> ▶ *You think an acquaintance would make a great friend and you'd like to know her better.*

When you want to get to know someone better, remember that everything in life has its own pace. You can ask the person to do something with you: "Would you like to go shopping Saturday?" If she says she can't, she may not like shopping so you could make another suggestion. If she turns you down again, and doesn't offer an alternative, she may not be ready for a new friendship.

> ▶ *You keep testing your friends to see if they will be trustworthy—sometimes they are, sometimes they aren't.*

When friends fail the tests you put out for them, it's probably your testing them that isn't working, not your friends. They don't have any obligation to live up to your expectations. Their job is to take care of themselves just as yours is to take care of yourself. They can help you enjoy your travels through life, but you have to keep yourself in good working order. If you want to apologize, say, "I was pushing too hard for you to take care of me and I'm sorry. From now on, I'm going to accept you as you are and take care of my own problems."

FRIENDSHIPS EBB AND FLOW

Rarely do relationships stay the same. Sometimes they are very intimate and at other times there is distance. Expecting a relationship to stay the same leads to a sense of loss and subsequent grief when it is less intense. Trying to hold a relationship at the same level of intensity also causes a great deal of strain and is likely to damage it, sometimes permanently.

YOU'VE GOT THE POWER

The going and coming of intensity is partly a natural phenomenon. People's lives change constantly with distractions and other interests moving into them. There may be nothing wrong between the people. But it may take time and some attention from each person to readjust the relationship.

Of course, there are times when the distance or tension that shows up in a relationship is due to hurt feelings, anger, or jealousy. It's a good idea to check out the reasons. Just hope that the other person will be honest.

The biggest problem comes when feelings get hurt when distance shows up in the relationship and is allowed to continue. The assumptions made can drive a wedge between the two people. This problem can be avoided by patiently backing off in order to give the person who needs distance the time to do whatever needs to be done before returning to the relationship. Know that if there is health and value in the relationship, it *will* continue over time.

WHAT TO DO AND SAY

▶   *You notice your old high school friend, who has called you monthly for a long talk, stops calling.*

Noticing that an old friend is no longer calling raises two possibilities: (1) Your friend thinks you said or did something that caused hurt feelings; or (2) Your friend is involved elsewhere and simply does not have time right now to continue the relationship as before.

Tell your friend you notice a difference. Preferably do this as soon as you notice it, so you do not make a lot of assumptions and become hurt or angry.

Ask your friend whether you have done or said something that was offensive. If your friend says, "Yes," you are fortunate and can clear up whatever the problem is. If your friend says, "No," say reassuringly, "Please be honest with me. It's okay if you're mad at me. I never intentionally hurt you." At this point, you are at the mercy of your friend's psychological courage and honesty.

If your friend still says "No," ask if there is something else in the person's life. Reassure your friend that you don't have to know what that is. After all, it could be anything from falling in love, to having marriage problems, or going into bankruptcy. Your friend may be feeling shame and may not want anyone to see those feelings. Say, "Is there something else? I don't need to know *what* it is. Just know I care. You mean a lot to me."

Tell your friend, "I'll be there for you in whatever way you want. I'll help or stay out of your way until you ask me." Now that's a really good friend!

▶ *You view yourself as a loyal friend but find you are less interested in spending time with an old friend since you got divorced.*

If you are the one losing interest in a friendship, be kind. Tell your friend, "You have done nothing wrong. I am just finding myself overwhelmed, or pulled in other directions right now. I need to back away for a while. I would appreciate your understanding."

If you are involved with someone who has major problems with feelings of abandonment or separation, that person may try to hang on. You may need to say, "I am sorry I cannot be there for you now, but I *must* back off. I don't wish to hurt you, but I *must* do this for myself." If that still doesn't do the trick, you may need to point out that the person is jeopardizing any hope for a reconnection of the friendship in the future.

Be willing to let go of the friendship, for a time, whenever it suits either one of your needs.

OPEN YOUR EYES— NEW FRIENDS ARE THERE

If you're having a hard time making new friends, perhaps you're setting up unrealistic requirements. Instead of looking for *one* perfect person who meets all your qualifications, you could meet a handful of people who each have some of those qualities you're looking for—and maybe a lot more to offer. Besides, there are plenty of fascinating, fun people in the world, who may live in a different neighborhood, belong to another religion, have a different skin color, or income level. Don't let differences like these keep you from exploring new friendships.

YOU'VE GOT THE POWER

When you're looking for friends, ask yourself this: "How good am I at being a friend?" Instead of searching for people to fulfill *your* needs, be supportive of others in your life. Find ways to uplift those around you with a bright manner and sincere compliments. Give a hand to those who are helping themselves to the best of their ability but who could use a kind word.

Once you stop looking for friends who can fulfill *your* needs and start being a friend to others, you'll be amazed at how much richer your life will be.

WHAT TO DO AND SAY

▶ *You've just moved to a new city and don't know anyone.*

When you move to a new city, stay in touch with your old friends. But be prepared—long-distance relationships are hard to maintain. Your friends may not reciprocate. Use the ones who do for support when you're lonely, but focus on your new location and job, and what they have to offer.

You are given opportunities to make friends wherever you go. Start a conversation with someone in the bookstore or library about what they're reading. Ask someone questions in the grocery store about a new product or how they like to cook a dish. See if the groups you belonged to before have affiliated ones in your new city. Check out any support groups for new arrivals from the Chamber of Commerce.

You'll feel more at home if you pick certain stores, repair shops, and restaurants that you like and go there regularly. Find out the names of the people behind the counter so that you'll be greeted when you come in. Introduce yourself to your neighbors, and invite them to come over for a visit. Keep your options and your mind open.

▶ *Your old friends are no longer as supportive and now you'd like to meet some new friends.*

Seek new friends on the basis of their actions, not on how they look. If you're concerned that you'll pick unsupportive friends again, remember we sometimes outgrow our old friends or simply go on to different interests. Since like attracts like, your positiveness will appeal to those who are also positive and healthy.

▶   *You're in a new job and would like to have the same kind of camaraderie with your coworkers that you had in your old job.*

Camaraderie at work doesn't happen overnight. It takes time and trust. You became that way with your old buddies through shared experiences and that is what will happen again. Be friendly and look for chances to be helpful, but you'll do better if you relax and let it all fall into place. It will happen, but it can't be forced. It takes a while for a group to completely accept a newcomer, and trying to force it might actually do more harm than good.

Be careful about trying to duplicate previous experiences. Let the new group take on its own identity.

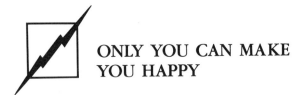

ONLY YOU CAN MAKE YOU HAPPY

Happiness is not an ultimate destination, it's a state of mind. Happiness isn't what you do, it's how you think. It isn't something to be earned in the future. Believe it or not, you *don't* automatically become happy when you reach your long-dreamed-of goal.

You can be happy whenever you want by appreciating what you have in this very moment.

What you believe affects your perception of what is around you. If you resolve to see the joy in everyone and everything, then you will. If you decide to find something beautiful in every day, then that is what you will see.

It all comes back to you. You can make yourself happy by first wanting happiness and then changing your thoughts to match. Your words and actions will follow.

YOU'VE GOT THE POWER

Make a commitment to think "happy."

☐ Check out the language you use. Get rid of negatives like, "I can't" and "I should," and replace them with, "I want to" and "I will." When someone compliments you, don't blow it off or put yourself down. Say, "Thank you, I really appreciate your noticing that."

☐ Find other positive people to be around. If you do have to be around unhappy types, visualize a protective blanket around you to keep their attitudes from rubbing off on you.

☐ When you are doing anything ask yourself, "Is this what I want to be doing? Is this making me happy?" If not, look for a way to improve the situation or find a more suitable opportunity.

WHAT TO DO AND SAY

▶ *You've finally achieved the job you've always wanted, but you aren't any happier after reaching your goal.*

First, congratulate yourself on your new position. Then realize that no job is perfect and they all have their assets and drawbacks. This one though may give you a chance to use some of your skills that others haven't. You can find happy moments in it, but don't make your job your life. Develop relationships and interests outside of work that nurture and stimulate you. You'll find yourself more fulfilled by your work if you're not expecting it to be everything for you.

▶ *You're working hard at your financial goal so you'll feel secure and happy later. Now, your life is an emotional desert because you don't have time to spend with anyone.*

It rarely pays to trade happiness now for security later because you may end up regretting the time and experiences you lost with others. Money can never replace special moments or your inner security because money can vanish. Once you're happy with whatever you're doing, the money will seem less important. Give yourself the most valuable gifts: love, time, and attention for yourself and the people who matter to you.

▶ *Mr. Right finally came along and life is better, but you're still not as happy as you thought you'd be.*

No matter how perfect someone is or how much he loves you, that person can't replace the love you need to give to yourself. Fill the gaps in your own heart, heal old hurts, decide to be happy, and then you'll truly be able to appreciate the wonderful person you've chosen.

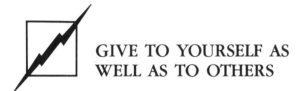

GIVE TO YOURSELF AS WELL AS TO OTHERS

Many people tend to take care of others rather than face their own needs. It is a lot easier for them to tell others what to do than to take responsibility for their own problems. Sticking our noses in other's business is tempting, but cheats the other person of independence and self-responsibility. It also doesn't work because you can't fix them or they, you. Parents are especially susceptible to this problem.

YOU'VE GOT THE POWER

Even when you have to be a caregiver it is important to take care of yourself. After all, you are the instrument of your caregiving and if you lose your sharp edge, you cannot do the job effectively. You're likely to feel impatience, irritability, and burnout when your well runs dry. On the other hand, self-care leads to a healthy, happy caregiver who has a lot to offer.

WHAT TO DO AND SAY

▶   *You stretch yourself to bake a batch of chocolate chip cookies and find yourself irritated
when your kids don't thank you.*

Don't do things for your kids that you think you
should (but don't really want to) do. Other than bare
necessities (which does not include chocolate chip
cookies) take care of yourself first so that you share
a happy, fulfilled parent with them. That is your children's greatest gift. Tell your kids, "Chocolate chip
cookies and a tired parent add up to bad news. I'll
make them when I feel rested." Your kids will understand because they *know* what you're like when
you're tired.

▶   *Your parents insist in jumping in to do things
for you even when you've asked them not to.*

When parents want to do things for you that you
don't ask for or need, tell them, "Thank you for thinking of me, but I'd rather do it myself." If they do
things for you anyway or without asking, say, "Thank
you for thinking of me but I'd rather you let me do
things for myself." And then, if they become angry
because of your ingratitude, say, "It's okay to be angry, but I must insist on doing things for myself."

▶   *You find yourself feeling resentful when you
cover for your loved one's behavior from the
night before.*

To your loved one, say, "I will no longer take responsibility for your behavior. I won't cover for you anymore." That's all you have to say. Then go about

developing your independence and give responsibility for your spouse *to* your spouse. You may, in addictive situations, need to request an intervention with a professional to further confront your loved one, if he does not take responsibility for his own behavior.

▶   *On Friday afternoon you're just finishing your own project after a tough week. You're looking forward to going home to your waiting family when a coworker asks you to help out because he got behind after taking a couple of long lunches earlier in the week.*

Say "No" to your coworker who asks for help because of irresponsibility. You can do this by saying, "I'm sorry I can't help you, but I have previous plans." Don't take responsibility to fix what he messed up. There also is no need to lecture, scold, or point out that he should have watched his time more carefully earlier in the week. There also is no need for you to make big excuses for why you can't help. Keep it simple.

YOU REALLY *DO* DESERVE PRAISE

If no one notices that you're doing a great job, don't get mad, and don't keep waiting for someone to mention it. Give yourself compliments at every opportunity. Who knows the words you want to hear more than you do?

Your happiness does not have to depend on what those around you do or say. You wouldn't be able to fulfill all of their needs and they couldn't satisfy yours. So take charge of your feelings. Determine that you will stay excited about your life because you're always hearing how wonderful it is from the true authority—you.

YOU'VE GOT THE POWER

Before you go to bed, review the day's happenings and congratulate yourself for things you did well that day. Say, "I really feel good about the way I did _____," or "I'm really glad I spoke up and said _____."

- ☐ Keep a file with your name on it. Write down supportive statements anyone makes to you and cut out sayings that uplift you. Read them often.

- ☐ When you do make a mistake, correct it and forgive yourself quickly.

WHAT TO DO AND SAY

▶ *Your family doesn't acknowledge the things that you do for them.*

If you're being taken for granted, maybe you're doing too much. Don't automatically do everything— wait until you are asked for help. Delegate tasks. See if the other kids' parents can help with carpooling and meetings. Then let go of the need to be a superparent. If you'd like more appreciation, say, "I really like it when you thank me when I do something for you." Their attitude will probably change once they are reminded of how much you do.

> ▶ *One negative comment—no matter how
> small—makes you feel low all day.*

Perfectionists tend to forget all the things they do right and only remember the things they do wrong. If you received a negative comment, keep it in perspective. Remind yourself that no one is perfect, and that you can't please everyone all of the time. Now remember all the things that went well on that same day, and don't place so much importance on what others think or say about you.

> ▶ *At work, you only get noticed when you do
> something wrong.*

Point out your accomplishments to your boss and coworkers. You could say: "I really feel good about getting this project done today!" or "We're going to be so much farther ahead because this project was finished this week!"

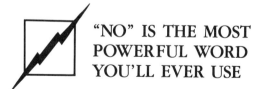

"NO" IS THE MOST POWERFUL WORD YOU'LL EVER USE

The most emotionally powerful word available to any of us is "No." It surrounds us with a defensive system that secures our boundaries, and it deflects unwanted intrusions. It allows us to be in charge of ourselves.

It takes emotional power to say "No." This power was first developed, if you can believe it, at the age of four. You may, however, have been punished for saying "No" when you were young. So, you may now have to learn how to get comfortable using the word.

In addition, the problem with emotional power is that it tends to come out in a rather chaotic fashion unless limits are applied to it. Much like a fire that rages out of control, power, too, can be hurtful. But a fire contained in a fireplace serves a purpose.

It is necessary to learn to modulate power so it can be firm, strong, and controlled. One way to do this is to use words to express power, and "No" is the king of these words.

YOU'VE GOT THE POWER

There are many ways to say "No" in addition to the bluntness conveyed with only the two letters. There are times when immediacy or urgency require the blunt form. But you may wish to use a variation:

"I prefer not to do that right now."

"I won't be able to do that for you."

"I'm not up to it now. Could you ask me later?"

"It isn't in my best interest to do that now."

"I can't let myself do that now."

☐   When someone does not want to take "No" for an answer, say, "I'm sorry you're having a hard time hearing me say 'No.' But I do mean it and pressuring me won't help. I can only do what I can do, or am willing to do."

☐   Once you say, "No," it is imperative that you stick with it unless presented with substantial new information that changes the picture. Otherwise you'll get a reputation for being wishy-washy and you will be pushed endlessly to convert your "No" to a "Yes."

☐ If you agree to think over a proposition, it is a good idea to tie yourself down to a time when you will get back to the person. Employees appreciate it. Kids need something definite. And it makes friends feel good.

WHAT TO DO AND SAY

▶ *At the very time you are busiest, you are asked to chair a committee at your kid's school.*

Being asked to do something when you are already overcommitted requires a "No" answer as the only responsible thing to do. You can say, "I can't hold the committee chair now, as I'm overcommitted and that wouldn't be a responsible thing for me to do."

You don't even need a reason other than, "I don't want to take the appointment," or "I don't like to head up committees."

▶ *Your employee asks for a raise. You don't want to lose that person but you also know the money is not in the budget.*

To your employee, say, "I want to get the money for you but it's not in the budget. Is there something else you want that we could negotiate, or could we talk about it again in a few months?"

▶   *Your child wants to have friends spend the
     night but you have to go to work the next
     morning.*

With children, you might tell them, "I want to help
you get what you want but by pushing me, it makes
me not want to even try later." It will help a lot to be
specific with the planning. Say, "Next Friday would
be a good time. I don't have to work the next day."

▶   *Your partner asks you to try something new
     sexually, but you're uncomfortable with the
     idea he brings up.*

It probably took a lot of courage on his part to
suggest something new sexually. He is risking rejection, or the possibility that you might think he's
strange. Don't be insulted; it's a compliment that you
can be trusted.

As gently as possible, say, "I wouldn't feel comfortable doing that." Reassure him that you care for
him. Say, "Even if I'm uncomfortable with an idea, I
still want you to tell me about it as long as you don't
pressure me into doing anything."

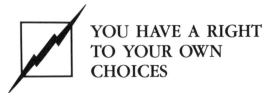

YOU HAVE A RIGHT
TO YOUR OWN
CHOICES

The great part about being a healthy human being
is that you can make choices, big and little, about
how you run your life. Yet some people will take it

upon themselves to question you about those decisions. And out of politeness, shock and/or sheer self-defense, you may think you need to answer them. You don't. You have a right to your own preferences and you don't have to justify them to anybody.

You might be in step or out of step with the mainstream, but it doesn't mean that you can't think for yourself or that you're rebellious. It does mean that the path you've chosen makes you happy for now. When it isn't working for you anymore, you will make another choice and find something that will. Remember, you get to define what you like.

YOU'VE GOT THE POWER

If you have the urge to change your image in some way but stop yourself with the words, "No, really, I shouldn't," ask yourself why.

Often the answer boils down to, "I care what other people think, and I'm afraid they'll laugh at me, or criticize me, or in some way I'll stand apart."

These were serious issues when we were teens, aligning ourselves with a special group of friends as a way to assert our individuality to our family. Usually that group had a strict dress and behavior code we dared not break.

As adults we tend to belong to a number of different groups simultaneously—the people we know at work, our friends, service organizations, our church, our family. We don't get along with every member of every group we belong to, and what that means is the groups are flexible, and accept a wide variety of individuals and behaviors.

So dare to be a little bit different, if it suits you.

Once you change that look, that habit, or the way you do things, enjoy the feeling of personal power that comes from making your own choice. Who knows, you may start a trend!

WHAT TO DO AND SAY

▶   *You change your eating habits and someone questions you about them.*

If you have quit drinking, or quit eating red meat or sugar and someone asks about it, don't try and explain. For some reason, most people will take it as a challenge and tell you why you're wrong. You'll end up justifying your decision and feeling bad about something you know is good for you. Simply say, "I don't like sweet things/alcohol/red meat (etc.)."

If they ask again, just repeat it. Believe it or not, a simple statement like this will shut people up.

▶   *You dress unusually and people ask why.*

If they question why you do something like wear stripes with plaids, just smile and say, "I like stripes and plaids."

▶   *At work, you have a different but more effective way of doing tasks but are told you should do it like everyone else.*

If you do tasks at work differently from the others, say, "I'm more comfortable doing it this way."

If it's not affecting coworkers but they comment about it anyway, you may just want to laugh it off.

If your boss wants more explanation, say, "I get more work done this way. Could I show you how I do it and maybe it might help some other people?"

Then keep making those decisions that fit you!

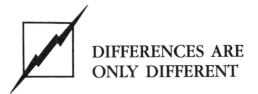

DIFFERENCES ARE
ONLY DIFFERENT

Differences between two people often act as impediments to their relationship. People often attempt to negate their differences and emphasize their similarities in the mistaken belief that this will draw them closer to each other.

To cope with the feelings of discomfort that the awareness of differences can sometimes bring, you may view similarities as "good" and differences as "bad." Introducing a value judgment, however, does away with the richness of diversity and sets up two camps: one for the good guys and one for the bad. It also sets up a situation where there is a winner in the relationship, and also a loser. When that happens, distance is the inevitable result—and all because differences have been denied or go unresolved.

Yet all one has to do is see differences for what they are: only differences. Take the judgment out of the situation and you can have two people whose points of view are both right. It is only a matter of looking at the world from the perspective of the other person. Doing so does not mean you have to abandon your

perspective. You can keep your view while understanding another's. Then you have two experiences
available to enrich your life and all you have to do is
share those experiences, not judge them.

YOU'VE GOT THE POWER

Ask yourself how the differences between you and
another person matter. In most cases the answer will
be, "They don't." They will turn out to be only a
matter of preference.

☐ Ask the other person to describe how he or
   she feels, and why. Be sure to ask a sincere
   question, otherwise your request will be
   communicated as a demand or challenge and
   will shut down communication, not open it.

☐ Explain how you feel and why you make the
   choices you are making. Say, "Here's how I
   feel. I choose as I do because . . . What
   goes into the choices you make?"

☐ Listen intently with an attitude of acceptance,
   no matter how different the other person's
   position seems. You will be surprised how
   much you can learn.

☐ If you hear something that appeals to you, do
   not hesitate to adopt it, but remember the
   point is not to achieve similarity.

☐ When it comes to an area that requires two of
   you to be able to join forces to achieve a certain outcome, you must learn to negotiate and

find a consenses rather than a compromise. With a consensus, you work until you find a point of resolution that makes each of you truly feel good. A compromise means that neither one of you gets what you want, and neither of you feels satisfied.

WHAT TO DO AND SAY

▶   *You like to make love* after *you have rested and your lover prefers sex* before *resting.*

Use a scale from one to ten to measure the extent of your desire. If you want to make love before you go to sleep but your desire is moderate (for example, it would be nice tonight but it's also okay in the morning), you might rate yourself at a five level. If you find that your spouse is exhausted after a grueling day and really needs to sleep, say, "I understand, sleep well." If you're the one who is tired, say, "After some rest, I'm sure my eagerness will return."

If each of you need, strongly, the opposite of what the other needs, look understandingly at each other and accept the other's need without requiring yourself to fulfill it. The one who doesn't want sex must not be forced, but can empathize reassuringly with the one who does. Say, "I understand and I love you. I would like to be able to meet your needs right now but I simply can't. Could I hold you instead?"

No judgments, cajoling, or force, no arguments, pressures, or heartaches are necessary. Just understanding.

▶   *You and your colleague work as a team, but you like a summer vacation and your colleague would rather vacation in the winter.*

Speak with your colleague with the understanding that neither of you is right or wrong, but you do have to find a solution. Brainstorm options: "One year we could take a summer vacation, a winter one the next." Or, "Could each of us work alone until the other gets back?" Keep discussing alternatives until you find one that suits you both.

▶   *You feel uncomfortable when someone condemns all members of an ethnic group.*

Being confronted by prejudicial attitudes is tough. It can be emotionally painful and cause feelings of helplessness. You can say, "My point of view is different—I tend to judge people on their individual merits." If the person questions you, continues to make insults about people, or begins to build a case, say more firmly, but slowly and precisely, "All people have value for me. Since you feel differently, there is no point in continuing our discussion on this subject. Let's talk about something else."

TREAT SPECIAL PEOPLE SPECIAL

Knowing people who love and care about you is one of the most important gifts life has to offer. These are the people who will be there when you are at your lowest or just need a helping hand. They will share your good times and provide support when you're afraid. These people deserve special treatment.

But we are often hardest on the ones closest to us. Maybe it's because we feel safer with them and don't fear rejection or retaliation. Maybe you are too tough on yourself and it's reflected in how you deal with others. Maybe it's just too easy to be critical when others don't live up to our expectations. Perhaps it's because we pressure others to make us happy and they continually fail. And they always will fail, because only you are responsible for your happiness.

YOU'VE GOT THE POWER

Take responsibility for meeting your own needs and be patient with yourself when you don't. When you do, you'll find it easier to treat special people like the special human beings they are.

When you make life easier for the ones you love, they will in turn make life easier for you by staying in your life. Examine your attitudes:

☐ If you pick a fight with one person because you are really angry at another, be honest and say, "I am sorry. I am really angry at X because . . ." Discuss the problem and give your loved one the chance to comfort you. When you think about it, that's what you really needed from the person you are with.

☐ Practice focusing your attention on the situation you are in. When you leave that situation, put it out of your mind. This way, you have answered your need to approach each part of your day with a fresh, uncluttered mind.

☐ If you find that you are unduly imposing your standards on others, say, "I need to loosen up. What matters is that the job gets done, not the way people do it."

☐ If you expect other people to make you happy, ask, "What am *I* doing to make *them* happy? The more I give, the more I will get what I need."

WHAT TO DO AND SAY

▸ *All of the romance is out of your relation-ship and you find yourselves bickering constantly.*

You may have picked your partner for a number of reasons from how good you felt when you were around him or her to how perfect that person seemed for you. But no one is perfect nor does anyone stay the same. You can ride out your mistakes and changes and discover new and exciting aspects of each other or you can let your disappointment eat away at your love until there is nothing left.

A relationship is about sharing experiences, not filling the holes inside of you, many of which only you can fix. Realize that your partner is with you by choice. Be flattered by that choice and show your appreciation. Look for reasons to give each other compliments. Leave notes on one another's pillows or in books. Give and ask for lots of hugs. Tell your partner that it's okay to both give and accept these gestures. Go on dates and take turns bringing each other flowers. Take your partner dancing or for a walk in the park. Talk about your dreams with each other without any pressure to make them happen. When you're having rough times, share a joke or a smile together, and you may be amazed at how much smoother things will feel.

▶   *You have a close friend you don't see very
    often and who now seems to be distant when
    you do get together.*

With a good friend, you may still feel a close connection, but since you don't see each other so often, that person may want a little more attention from you. If you feel distance when you talk, say, "I know we haven't spent much time together lately because I've been busy. Let's make a date for lunch or "Let's set up a time to get together soon."

If you can't get together more, staying in touch on the phone or through notes will help to keep your relationship alive.

▶   *As a boss, you find yourself taking advantage
    of your best employee.*

If you're taking advantage of an employee, you may not want that person or anyone else to know how much you depend on him because it makes you feel vulnerable. Tell yourself, "This person does not threaten me because I am very capable. He or she only helps me to do a better job." You may be afraid good employees will leave if they know how valuable they are. But they'll be more likely to want to stay if you're occasionally telling them how important they are to you and the company. Simply say, "I appreciate the work you do. I'm glad I can count on you."

▶   *Your kids are fussing more than usual.*

When your children are fussing more than usual, they may want some individual attention from you. When you go to the store, you could specifically ask one of them to come along. You could hire a sitter for the others or have your spouse watch them and take one out to dinner or for a walk. If one is crying while you're on the phone, pull him up on your lap and see if he doesn't want to get down as soon as he's assured of your attention.

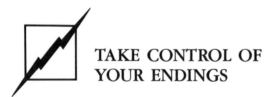

TAKE CONTROL OF YOUR ENDINGS

As we move through life, there are people and situations that we leave behind as we grow and change. Friendships will end when two people no longer have something to give to each another. Relationships break apart when they have fulfilled their function or there is a more effective or efficient way to meet the needs of the people involved. Jobs are outgrown as our skill levels increase or our goals change. Schools and the people who run them are left behind as we move into the work world.

The way in which we separate from these situations and people makes a lot of difference in the quality of our lives. Sometimes separations are facilitated by picking a fight, which makes it easier to leave. The problem with this approach is that it generates a lingering resentment that may cause damage later.

Bad mouthing, impulsive leaving, and angry exits that blame others for real or imagined slights all wreak havoc. Realizing that relationships and situations come to an end and that this is not necessarily anyone's fault will help the transition. Grieving over the loss instead of pointing a finger and blaming others will lead to a faster recovery.

Just as litter mars the landscape, so does emotional litter mar our path through life. Keep those paths clean and you will experience a more beautiful life; one where you can return to places already visited and people already known should you sometime want to in the future.

YOU'VE GOT THE POWER

Monitor your feelings as you live out your life. Each day, resolve to make peace with the people and the situations you confront. Do not ignore problems because they don't tend to go away.

☐ Say, "Thank you," for what you gain out of every situation and then, if you must, say goodbye to it. Your goodbyes may be temporary or they may be permanent, but you will not know that at the time. Leave with grace.

☐   Respect the fact that each of us does the best we can at any given moment, then go on from there free from blame for another and for yourself.

WHAT TO DO AND SAY

▶   *You realize it is time to end your relationship.*

When you depart from a relationship, it's important to realize that you had a role in the selection of your mate, no matter how bad the person seems to you now. You also have a role in the ending of the relationship. Say, "I accept responsibility for my part in all of this mess and I give you your part of the responsibility. But, it is time for us to go our separate ways."

If you are angry or hurt, tell your partner about it and then let it drop—no matter what his or her response is. If you are unable to confront your partner or feel it is unwise, you can write a letter that you never mail. Say all the things that are going on in your mind. Then say goodbye to the part of you that was involved in the situation.

▶   *You have outgrown your position at work.*

When leaving a job, say, "I've appreciated working for you." or "I've gained a great deal working for you." Then, "It's time to move on to a new goal that I want to go after. Thanks for everything."

▶   *It is time for you to leave school and enter the work force. You are now an adult.*

When moving through one of life's transitions, such as graduation, marriage, parenthood, children leaving home, or retirement, take the time to review the ground you've covered. It's even useful to get downright nostalgic. Briefly reexperience the good and tough times. If you have any unfinished business, take care of it now. Write out your feelings, if you can't talk directly to the people involved.

You may even experience some grief as you let go of the old. That's fine. Then welcome your future and plan your next steps. Tell yourself, "I'm ready to meet my future. I will do the best job I know how to do with it. And I look forward to it."

YOU CAN BE FREE OF YOUR PAST

You may have made a lot of mistakes in your relationships in the past. It isn't that you don't deserve better or that it was bad luck, you just learned to make poor choices. Now you are picking people who treat you the way you want to be treated. But the key to happiness is in letting go of those past relationships so they won't haunt your new ones.

Instead of focusing on how alike a present situation is to one in your past, you need to concentrate on trusting your own judgment. If you feel you've done all this before and are trapped again, it's most likely self-doubt rearing its ugly head.

Ask yourself: "Is this a legitimate concern or is something in this situation triggering my fear that since I couldn't get what I wanted in the past, I might not get it now?"

If you note similarities to the past in your current situation, it doesn't automatically mean you've made another wrong choice. Examine the situation again, this time noticing the differences to the past. If there are significant differences, *you* may just be repeating the same pattern with a new person. Use it as an opportunity to break the cycle.

If you're involved with someone with any kind of an addiction, maybe you just want to say "No" to that kind of life and realize that you can do it.

YOU'VE GOT THE POWER

Tell yourself, "I deserve the best and I'm making choices to that end."

☐ After reassuring yourself, look clearly at the other person. If you really are repeating the same pattern with no hope of working this out either, then let it go. You could say: "I can't get what I need from you and that's so important to me that I need to end this relationship."

☐ It's okay to keep an eye on any new people to see if some of your old problems are repeating with them. But the emphasis needs to be on you! Instead of pointing out what they are doing wrong, look at what is upsetting you, and why.

WHAT TO DO AND SAY

▶ *Your first husband wouldn't help with the housework, and now your present husband is slacking off.*

Discuss your feelings with him; articulate what you need. "I'm upset because I need help with the housework and it's not being done. How can I help you help me?" Talk about your past fears but don't drag up all the gory details. Your spouse may be so upset by your comparison that he won't hear anything else.

You could say, "I've been in a situation like this before where I never was able to get what I needed and I'm afraid it's happening again." That gives him the chance to say he wants to work with you, and a chance for each of you to come up with ideas to solve the problem.

▶ *A former friend used to subtly put you down and now you're listening for the same in a new friend.*

If you hear something that you think is a put-down or that you're confused about, you might say, "My feelings were a little hurt by something you said. I might have heard it wrong. Could you explain it to me?"

▶ *A coworker has stolen some of your ideas and now you're afraid to brainstorm with anyone.*

If you're afraid to trust others, you may be afraid to trust yourself. Acknowledge the soundness of your judgment and then listen carefully as your inner voice tells you who is trustworthy and who is not.

GRIEF IS A NATURAL PART OF LIFE

Grief is the normal reaction to any loss. It may be the loss of a loved one, a dream, a job, or old ways. Even when change comes along to better your life, you will feel the loss of familiar territory.

Grief is a process that has several stages: First is denial, which is characterized by, "I can't believe this is happening to me." Second is anger at and about what happened: "It's not fair. God abandoned me." Anger is protection against the pain of the loss. The third stage is one of bargaining in which we try to strike a deal to either avoid the loss or nullify it. Guilt is a characteristic of this stage: "If only I had . . . it wouldn't have happened." Stage four is depression. By the time this feeling hits, you are allowing the loss to truly sink in and you are feeling a lot of emotional pain. It is the time when true goodbyes are said and old business is finished in our minds with the object of our loss.

When these four stages are completed, the fifth and final stage, called acceptance, can fall into place. It is an adjustment to the new reality of life with the loss as a matter of fact. And life goes on. Of course, there will be remembrances of the loss, especially at anniversary times, but by and large, you will come through it.

Getting stuck in a grief reaction only happens when there is unfinished business either with the object of the loss or with something from the past that reminds you of the loss. For example, if you felt angry at your father but did not have the opportunity to resolve that anger before he died, you will tend to continue to grieve until you have a chance to resolve it. If you suffered the loss of a dream because you allowed someone, against your better judgment, to talk you out of it, you are likely to stay depressed until you become strong enough to no longer be susceptible to pressure from other people.

With major grief, it tends to take two years to work through to the acceptance stage. That is why people are advised to refrain from making major decisions, including forming romantic bonds, for two years after a divorce or the death of a spouse. It is also best to delay changing your residence, or buying or selling a business, because the world will look quite different after your grief is healed.

YOU'VE GOT THE POWER

When you first experience a loss, become very selfish and take good care of yourself. Do what you want to do as long as it is not unhealthy; i.e., drowning your sorrow in alcohol only delays your feeling the grief. It is still there. Talking with someone about your feelings will help. When you are ready, reach out to someone else who is comfortable with hearing about feelings. You do not need to make apologies for how you feel, nor do you need to be told that you "shouldn't" feel or act in a certain way.

☐ Become familiar with the stages of grief and track your own experience. Use a journal to write down what you feel, when you feel it.

☐ Give yourself time to heal. Don't run away from what happened or try to bury yourself in work. On the other hand, go on at a moderate pace with your life, even though you're functioning at a fairly low level.

☐ Ask for a shoulder to cry on—literally.

☐ Ask coworkers to cover for you at work. Be sure to let your boss know what you are going through. Most bosses are sympathetic and understanding.

☐ Know that you are not going crazy and recognize that although the feelings surrounding grief can be very strong, they are normal. If you become frightened by your feelings, be sure to talk with a counselor to gain reassurance that you are really okay.

☐ Eat, sleep, and exercise regularly even though you may not want to and may do so poorly. And above all do not isolate yourself, but reach out to others who have been down the path ahead of you. It's time to call in your markers and ask for as many favors as you need.

☐ Ask yourself what you can learn from what is happening.

☐ Know that your period of grief *will* end.

WHAT TO DO AND SAY

▶   *Someone close to you dies.*

When a spouse or loved one dies, realize that your whole life will change. Later, you will recover. Draw upon your friends, your family, and your faith, and follow the steps in grieving. If you get stuck, ask for help. Counselors are available who are trained to help you work through your grief.

▶ *A close friend moves away.*

When a close friend moves, don't be surprised when you go through quite a grief reaction. Depending on how deep the friendship, you may feel as if a part of you is gone. Follow the same guidelines as you would for the death of someone you love. Don't be ashamed to grieve, though you may not get as much sympathy as when a person dies. But some people will understand. Say to yourself, "This, too, will pass."

▶ *You worked hard on your first job, doing all that was asked of you, more than many others who worked there for a long time. Yet you are the first person laid off when business went down.*

If you are confronting the first big loss in your life, it is likely to hit you very hard. You may find out that life will not always treat you fairly. This leaves a double dose of loss on you. Tell yourself that you really are okay and that you will get over this loss. Say, "I am building character."

At work there is rarely any value in telling off bosses. Even though you got laid off, you can still get a recommendation, and probably a good one, because you did good work. If you blow up, you jeopardize that networking capability. Instead, share your angry feelings with someone outside the work place.

Then go get another job. Your good work habits will pay off.

> ▶ *You suffer repeated losses over a short period of time and seem unable to recover.*

If you have endured multiple losses in quick succession, tell yourself that the situation is temporary. Your entire life will not be like this, although it feels that way and you may want to give up. Also, drop everything that is not essential to your existence and concentrate on nurturing yourself. Quit fighting letting go of control over what is happening and attend to your needs. Multiple losses mean your recovery will take longer, that's all.

Ask yourself what you can learn from what is happening.

Know that your period of grief *will* end.

> ▶ *You go out of your way to do everything you can to make the evening exceptional for a special date, and he says he's too busy to see you the next week. You really expected a different outcome.*

When you want to put yourself out for another person, it's a good idea to make sure of your motives. If you are trying to pay another to have a relationship, stop. Let the relationship develop on its own. There will be plenty of time for spending money later as a reflection of a nicely unfolding togetherness. When you've already overspent, learn from what you're doing as you grieve the outcome of your mistake.

ANGER IS A COVER-UP EMOTION

When you get angry, you may assume it's because you are upset about what someone has done to you. You may want to pay them back or you may take your rage out on someone else. It's hard to see beyond the moment: you're consumed with thoughts of revenge or thoughts of the wrong. But there may be something deeper going on besides your anger at the actions of others. Anger is often a cover-up emotion. It's such a powerful feeling that it can disguise what's really going on inside you.

When someone hurts you, you may really be feeling powerless to protect yourself and afraid that it will happen again. Or when your trust is betrayed, you may really be sad at the loss of someone you thought you could rely on. Now you may be worried you can't trust your judgment and new people. It's vital that you know the truth about yourself because it's the only way you can fix the situation. Otherwise, you end up doing battle with something you can't change: the behavior of other people.

YOU'VE GOT THE POWER

Keep the focus on yourself by taking responsibility for your behavior. You choose what your reactions are and can therefore make another choice about how to express your anger.

☐ Let anger out in positive, harmless ways: count to ten while taking slow, deep breaths; leave the room; stamp your feet. Then ask yourself:

Why am I upset?

Am I frustrated?

What need isn't being taken care of?

How can I get what I want?

WHAT TO DO AND SAY

▶ *Other people—children, employees—make you mad when they won't do what you want.*

When others won't do what you want, remind yourself that the only behavior you can change is your own. Let them fix their own problems. Quit telling them what to do and devote the time to working on yourself.

If you're a parent or boss, ask what your child or employee needs to accomplish his/her tasks. "How can I help you?" is very effective. Helping the person learn problem solving skills is much better than telling someone what to do.

▶ *You get angry when anyone seems to put you down.*

If insults or even implied put-downs upset you, see if they are triggering any old messages you learned as a child. Tell yourself: "I am valuable. I don't deserve to be put down." Use your anger as a sign that you need to keep recording new, *positive* affirmations on the tapes that play in your head.

There are also people who are just obnoxious. Avoid them whenever possible.

▶ *You get upset when a loved one isn't taking care of her health.*

For someone who won't take care of his/her health, say: "It makes me sad that you won't take care of yourself, but I realize that I can't do anything to make you change your habits." Or write a letter with these words in it. Then recognize that your sad feelings are the only feelings you can take care of.

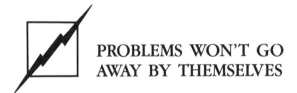

PROBLEMS WON'T GO AWAY BY THEMSELVES

When dirt is swept under the carpet rather than disposed of, it leaves a mound that in time turns into a hill that eventually becomes a mountain. Anytime you don't complete a job, it just hangs around making itself known at the worst possible moment.

The moral to all of this is that you can be in control of your life by taking care of your business thoroughly and completely. A job includes the completion of the task *and* cleaning up afterward.

Unfinished business has a tendency to trip us up when we least expect it. Sometimes years go by before we again see the signs of what we didn't do.

None of us escapes unscathed. The best advice is to put this book down right now and finish whatever you started earlier. Then, join us again.

YOU'VE GOT THE POWER

It is important to follow through on feelings that you have within yourself. Don't ignore them, hoping they will go away.

☐   It is crucial to take care of all aspects of your business—personal and professional— in a timely manner. Don't put off doing so because you are afraid, intimidated, self-conscious or for any other reason.

☐   When cleaning up a Big Mess, say, "I let things go too long. I apologize for that. Now I am ready to do whatever it takes to fix the problem." Radical surgery may be necessary.

WHAT TO DO AND SAY

▶   *You notice that your teenager is staying out most of the night during the summer. You worry about drinking and sexual activity. You do nothing with the hope that you're wrong and your teenager will be in control by the time school starts without your having to say anything.*

Immediately sit down with your teenager and say honestly what you know. Do not scold or lecture. Make "*I*" statements: "I know you are staying out very late. I suspect you're drinking and sexually active. I am worried that you are out of control." If your teen denies a problem, begins to argue, or accuses you of poking your nose where it doesn't belong, say firmly, "You can be mad, but I'm your parent and I'm worried. I respect you enough to try to discuss my concerns reasonably with you, and I'd like you to show me the same respect." Keep calm and encourage your child to talk to you by being silent long enough to give him or her a chance to respond. If he or she doesn't respond immediately, keep calm and be persistent. Encourage your teenager to bring friends home, and when school starts say, "I trust you to do what is in your best interest. I'll help you in any way you want."

If you don't get a constructive response, it's a good idea to seek outside help. Say, "I have already made an appointment with a family counselor. I need help in knowing what to do. I want you to go with me." If your son or daughter refuses, say, "I'm going anyway and will let you know what the next step is. If you want to have input into the decisions about you, then you need to come." Say no more but GO!

▶ *As a supervisor you have been noticing for a year that there is a lot of gossip in the hallways. It has made you uneasy, but you let it continue because you didn't know how to stop it. Now, your best employee is quitting because of it.*

It is important to be thorough with every job you do even when you don't like what you have to do. With gossipy employees, get the group together, using an outside consultant if necessary. Have employees voice their feelings. Assure them that it's safe to talk with no repercussions. (You must stand by your word on this point.) Encourage them to talk out their gripes, to tell you what they want and how they think low morale can be boosted. Brainstorm ways to accomplish the goals settled upon. Reinforce the program regularly and stop any gossiping immediately. Say, "Let's get your feelings out right now—I'll listen and then we can see what we can do."

▶   *You have been feeling uncertain in a personal relationship. Your friend isn't paying enough attention to you, but hasn't said anything. Now you can't even talk to the person without getting angry.*

When you and your partner start drifting away from each other, you might say, "This is hard to talk about, but I want to be clear about what each of us needs. I feel you are pulling away. That hurts me, but you are free and I don't want to hold you against your will." Then ask the big question, "Are you willing to work on our relationship with me?" If he says "No," or "There's nothing wrong," then you'll need to take a deep breath and begin to back out of the relationship, even if you don't want to do so. If he says, "Yes," but doesn't follow through, you need to confront the fact that your partner's behavior doesn't support the "yes" response. Backing off if this doesn't clear immediately is the only way to save your self-respect and self-esteem.

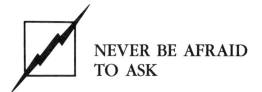

NEVER BE AFRAID TO ASK

There are few situations that can make you feel more powerless than when you can't solve a problem and don't know how to ask anyone else for help. You may have learned not to ask from your parents, who would get uncomfortable or wouldn't answer you at all when questioned. You may have heard from a teacher that you asked too many questions or disrupted the classroom when you were really trying to get help.

You may have been taught to be self-reliant and that it's a sign of weakness to reach out. Or your pride may get in the way because you believe you shouldn't need any kind of assistance.

The truth is, you are human. And every human being needs help at one time or another. You have a right to live your life as fully, easily, and happily as you want. The information to do that is rarely in just one person's head, but it is available. You just have to be willing to find it. The key to opening that door is in your helping yourself by asking others.

YOU'VE GOT THE POWER

Give yourself permission to be human.

☐ If you were taught not to ask, put new messages in your head: "I can ask for the answers

I need," "I am making myself stronger when I get help from someone else," or "My questions are important ones."

☐ Tell yourself: "What I need is available. All I have to do is look for it."

☐ If you don't want to start with the people you know personally, make use of libraries and bookstores. Practice asking for what you need with the librarians and clerks. Combined, they have information on everything on your subject, from reference books, to exposés, to magazine articles on microfiche. See if anyone at this store has an interest in your topic and a recommendation. The reference librarian may have a list of groups that have even more specific information, and volunteers who can talk to you one-on-one.

WHAT TO DO AND SAY

▶   *You've made a lot of mistakes at work and lost jobs because of them. Now you have a new position you really like and don't want to lose it.*

If you've made a lot of errors at work, it may be because the instructions weren't presented clearly. It probably has nothing to do with your intelligence but everything to do with your learning style (maybe you learn easier seeing information rather than hearing it, or vice versa) or the way you listen. Now it's time to start a habit of getting clarification on anything that doesn't make sense to you. Find someone who seems to understand and looks open to questions. When the orders are given in a group, ask that person, "Did I hear Ms. Smith say we need to do _____?" Then he can confirm it or say, "No, she said to do _____." If they are in a memo, you may want to ask: "Does this say we need to do _____?" When someone gives you directions, say, "I want to make sure I do this correctly. Did I hear you say _____?"

▶ *Your spouse is frustrated with you because you won't ask him for help. But everytime you do, he takes over and does the job for you.*

If you're not getting the kind of help you need, you may need to be more specific. If you need a listener, say "I'm trying to figure out a problem. Would you be willing to just listen while I talk about it out loud?" If you just want some suggestions, ask for them. If you need to be shown what to do, say, "Would you be willing to show me the first step and then I'll take it over from there?" If you need the task done for you, give yourself permission to ask, "Could you do this for me?"

If you believe that you need more information than your spouse can provide about an issue, don't hesitate to take advantage of the other people in your life. You can bring up the topic or ask, "Do you know anything about _____?" and you might be surprised how much you can learn without much effort. You can also call people in your field of interest and find out what they know and would recommend for you.

If he won't let you do it yourself, even when you have tried asking for his help, he's not hearing what you're really saying. It's important to start at square one. Put a stop to his work immediately. Let him know that this is something *you* want to do and you're only asking for his help. Be specific about what you want from him, even if it takes you longer to do the job. Say it with a smile so he understands you're not ungrateful or criticizing him.

▶ *You find yourself angry and resentful because you have too much on your shoulders at work and home.*

If you're burned out, delegate, delegate, delegate! Look for ways that you can get help from your boss, coworkers, and employees. Have what you need planned out. Then say, "I want to do the best job possible, so I'll need more assistance in these areas."

When you're burned out by family chores, say, "I can't do everything," and start assigning tasks. Then don't get upset when they aren't done as well as you would do them. Also, be willing to let some chores go and have some fun instead. You'll find yourself shouldering your responsibilities with a much lighter heart.

▶ *You want or need a recommendation.*

For a recommendation from someone you know well, just ask, "I need a recommendation. Would you be able to give me one?" If you don't know anyone well, make an appointment with someone who is approachable and say; "You're a well-respected person and I know you can't make a recommendation unless you know something about me, so I'd like to tell you about myself." Present your qualifications and make it easy for the person to talk to others about you. Underscore the points you want emphasized.

FIND YOUR FIT

Our uniqueness forms our identity. Just as a tulip bulb holds the specific elements of each tulip, there is the seed of this identity within each of us that holds all our potential. As that identity unfolds, we become what is within us.

While our life is unfolding, we travel through many experiences. Those experiences allow us to become more nearly who we are or to drift farther from the core of who we could be.

Each of us must take responsibility for our daily living. In the process of following our path, it is necessary to support ourselves. That job does not belong to anyone else. While you are doing that, you can keep your eye on your goal of fulfilling your identity. Each time you have the opportunity to make a choice, examine how you feel, and choose to do what fits you best.

If you don't honor your innate identity, then you're likely to become dissatisfied. You'll feel like you are simply existing and not really living. What you do will tend to yield money, rather than satisfaction.

Many midlife crises tend to come from not being in tune with our identity. Since we start facing our mortality in midlife, some people tend to get panicky that the "real" person will go undeveloped. At midlife especially, the thrust to fulfill our potential is strong.

YOU'VE GOT THE POWER

How do we know whether we are on the path that will most nearly allow us to unfold our identity? We experience each step of the travels as either feeling easy or difficult. Use that feeling as your guideline. When you're doing something that feels bad, you can bet you're off the track. It's that simple.

If you are dissatisfied, learn to analyze the sources of your dissatisfaction:

- ☐ Become aware of what you feel.

- ☐ Decide if you feel good or bad.

- ☐ When you feel bad, ask yourself what you were doing immediately before the feeling came.

- ☐ Be courageous by acknowledging what would fit you better.

- ☐ Give yourself permission to move to a position where you will feel better about what you are doing.

- ☐ Fend off other people who try to tell you what would be best for you by saying, "Thank you for your suggestion, but I will take responsibility for what I am doing." To a loved one whose life is tied to yours, say, "I love you but I must do what is best for me. I will also work with you so you can get what you need."

WHAT TO DO AND SAY

▶ *Though you were raised in a family with traditional roles, you're feeling stifled and frustrated when trying to do the same thing. You become more depressed every day.*

To a family member, you can say, "I am doing things differently from you. You are doing a good job with the life you have chosen, and I expect to do as well with my choice."

▶ *You were a successful teacher who loved what you did. Then you were promoted to an administrative job that you now hate.*

If you really hate it, then make arrangements to go back to teaching in the following school year. Generally, when you are successful, and like what you do, and then get offered a promotion in a different field, say, "I'm flattered and will give it a try but I want to be honest with you. If I don't feel satisfied, I'm going back to my old job."

▶ *You're moderately successful in what you do, but you really wanted to be in another career. You felt obliged to follow the career*

> *your family wanted for your because they felt*
> *much pride in what you would become. You*
> *have suffered from depression since you*
> *graduated.*

If someone tries to get you to do something that you don't feel fits you, say, "Thanks for the suggestion, but I'll take my chances doing what I want to do." You may be pressured to use special talents or skills. When someone says, "What a waste that you don't use your talents in science and math," you can say, "I know it must be hard to understand that I don't want to be a scientist, but I'm just not interested. I'm sure I'll do something that fits me."

 ## AN OCCASIONAL OVERINDULGENCE MAY BE GOOD FOR YOU

You have probably heard the old saying, "Do everything in moderation." That's also true of overindulgence. Overindulging will not automatically kill you—if you don't do it too often. As a matter of fact, an occasional overindulgence may be good for you.

Remember the harm isn't always in what you do but how (and how often) you do it. Being compulsive, for example, means that you feel compelled to do an activity and don't have any other choice. If you suspect you have that problem, seek out a counselor who can help.

On the other hand, letting yourself relax or do something different from your usual tight schedule could go a long way in relieving stress. It's healthy when you occasionally give yourself permission to overindulge, but you will want to consider the consequences beforehand and take responsibility for them.

YOU'VE GOT THE POWER

Give yourself permission to relax from your usual standards. Tell yourself: "I can let loose and enjoy myself and still be safe."

☐ If you plan to have several drinks when you go out, or exert yourself in an activity that will make you too tired to concentrate, make sure that you're physically safe and designate someone else as the driver.

☐ If someone else tries to pressure you into overindulging, you can simply say "No."

WHAT TO DO AND SAY

▶ *You're on a very strict low-calorie, low-fat diet but you really want a hot fudge sundae sometimes.*

If you're trying to lose weight, remember that many diets are designed to help you develop better eating habits. It doesn't mean you've blown it completely if you have an occasional hot fudge sundae.

Give yourself the treat and then get back on the program again. You'll be a lot happier and healthier than if you constantly feel deprived. The benefit of weight loss might be negated by the stress you've put yourself under by counting every single calorie, weighing out portions and denying yourself even a tiny bit of what you'd really like to eat.

If anyone sees you eating your treat and comments: "I thought you were on a diet!" reply, "I'm taking care of myself." If your friend persists, say, "That's really my business!"

▶   *Experts say you need to devote a certain
     number of hours to exercise to keep fit. You
     don't have that kind of time.*

Look at what the experts are saying. If you decide you should do some exercise, remember everybody is different.

Decide what purpose your program will serve: general health, building more muscle, weight loss or control.

See what exercises fit your goal.

Now look at your schedule and see how you can fit them in and how often.

Look for exercises you can do at your desk and when you're stuck in line. Instead of going out for lunch every day, you could go to the gym, for a walk or a run, and eat a healthy sandwich on the way back.

Ask friends and coworkers what they do to exercise. Look for books and magazine articles for more suggestions. Get an exercise machine or devise an exercise program you can do when you get up in the morning or while watching the evening news or your favorite programs. It's not important that you match the experts. It is important that you feel good about what you're doing.

▶ *Almost everyone in your field got ahead by working long hours of overtime. Now you're feeling pressured to do so, but you want to see your family more.*

Don't let yourself be pushed into working unnecessary overtime. Instead, see if you can work more efficiently during your regular working day. If someone asks why you aren't working longer hours, say: "I accomplish what I intend to during the hours I'm here." If you feel the need to put in some overtime, go to work an hour earlier. You'll still have the evening with your family.

If your career track and finances are affected, tell your family; "You are important to me and I want to spend time with you. We may not have as much money for the extra stuff but we will have lots of good times together."

LISTEN TO CRITICISM, THEN DO WHAT YOU WANT

Behind this reminder is the assumption that no one in the whole world knows better than you what is best for you. You get to be in charge of your whole life. You get to take the responsibility to run your life the way you want to, to monitor and evaluate what you do, and to choose how you do it.

So, when someone criticizes you, know that that is only one person's perception of a situation. You need not discount it nor do you need to accept it totally. Simply listen, and take time to glean any useful information from the person's input. Then integrate those points into your own agenda, acknowledging the person for her or his part while being clear in your own mind that you maintain control of what you do and how you do it.

Screen out any scolding, judging, or blaming. Screen out everything but the facts. People can let you know that there are alternative ways to do things but cannot tell you that their way is better and your way is worse. It doesn't matter whether the criticism was requested by you, foisted on you without your asking, or a part of a job. In all cases, the above guidelines apply.

If you were criticized, blamed, or scolded a lot as a child, you are likely to be extremely sensitive to these behaviors now. Realize that and work to eliminate the pain that is left over from childhood. You may benefit from a counselor to help you with this.

YOU'VE GOT THE POWER

When a person criticizes you personally, say, "Thank you for your concern, but I will handle it myself." Or perhaps you need to say, "I appreciate your concern, but I'll take responsibility for the outcome."

☐ Many times criticisms only have to do with individual differences—you don't do something the way your critic does. Recognize this criticism for what it is.

☐ If you are particularly susceptible to criticism, you need to remind yourself that you are no longer a child. In your mind, reach out to the vulnerable part of you that was personally hurt and comfort that part. See your critic as someone who needs to judge in order to feel strong because in reality they feel very weak.

WHAT TO DO AND SAY

▶ *Your spouse criticizes what you are wearing.*

If the criticism has to do with what you are wearing, say, "I'm sorry you are uncomfortable, but I like what I have on. If you wish, you don't need to go out with me." You're saying that you don't plan to change just because this person in uncomfortable. Remember, criticism is different from someone coming to you directly and saying, "Would you be willing to wear slacks to the wedding rather than jeans? I would feel better if you would." No judgments are being made in the latter situation and the choice is left up to you.

▶ *Your neighbor frowns disapprovingly and tells you, unasked, that you'll be sorry you let your children have as much independence as you give them.*

Always ask for specifics. Say, "What is it you are afraid of in my handling my children?" It is very likely your neighbor imagines your kids will be out of control as they grow up. Say, "The kids and I will take responsibility for their behavior."

▶   *Your supervisor rakes you over the coals,*
    telling you that your performance is awful
    and that you ought to get out of the business.

If a boss or anyone else is abusive to you, say, "You have good ideas that I'd like to hear. You don't need to be as forceful as you are to get your point across. I'm a good listener." If that doesn't do the trick, say, "Please put your criticisms in writing." And if you are still being overly criticized, say, "Stop. . . . I've got the message." Then leave.

FORGIVE YOURSELF WHILE YOU'RE TRYING TO CHANGE

Once you've recognized the areas in your life that you're dissatisfied with, you can begin to work to change yourself. But if it seems too hard or you're stuck, it may be because you're beating yourself up in the process. It's so important that you give yourself the time it takes to change.

You were taught what you *should* be like when you were very small and it made a big impression. It took a long time to learn what you know now and how to act in your own best interest. But when you're stressed out, challenged, or exhausted, it is easy to forget all of that and go back to the "shoulds." Chastising yourself will only make developing those new healthy habits take that much longer, because you'll be reinforcing those old negative messages. It's vital that you forgive yourself when you forget and momentarily fall into your old ways.

YOU'VE GOT THE POWER

☐ LIGHTEN UP! You will get better at remembering.

☐ Learn from your mistakes. You usually get more proficient by repetition so be grateful for your opportunities to practice!

☐ Applaud yourself when you do anything in the new way.

WHAT TO DO AND SAY

▶ *You're trying to stop gossiping but find yourself still doing it every time you meet a new person.*

Ask yourself: "Why do I want to gossip?" Maybe it's to distract you from your own problems. Maybe you feel people will like or respect you more because you always have the inside scoop. Maybe it's the only thing you have in common with certain people and you think they won't like anything else about you.

Gossiping may be a symptom just like drug or alcohol abuse. Take care of the feelings underneath and you may find the symptom going away. In a group, you can stay quiet and/or leave. With another person, say, "I don't know or want to talk about _____, but how are *you* doing?"

▶   *You want to talk calmly to your kids but can't seem to stop yelling.*

With your kids, you may be overtired. Arrange quiet time for yourself by getting someone to watch them, then go to the park or just lie down quietly. The old "count to 10" trick works a lot better when you're rested. If you have trained your kids to listen to you only when you yell, you'll need to train them again. Say, "I know you don't like yelling and I don't either, so I'm going to talk quietly now. But I need you to pay as much attention to my quiet voice as you did to my yelling." Then forgive them while you're forgiving yourself for however long it takes to change.

▶   *Your child is growing up and you need to give her more freedom. You're trying to let go of control but it's too dangerous.*

If you're scared to let go, remind yourself that you can't truly control everything in life. And the most control you have is over yourself, not someone else.

You may feel that you are losing your place in your child's life. Tell yourself, "I'm valuable even if I'm not needed the way I was before."

You also may have too much of your identity tied to being a mother. Say, "I'm more than a mother." Then, update your identity.

LONELINESS IS
A STATE OF MIND

By yourself? Disconnected? Adrift in the middle of a crowd? All of these are aspects of loneliness which is more a state of mind than a physical condition. It tends to be a feeling of lack of closeness, either physically or emotionally, to someone else. It is possible to be around people but feel isolated. If no one understands you or shares your interests, you're likely to feel alone. On the other hand, you may actually not have enough contact with other human beings to satisfy you.

Take a look at your situation. Do you push away opportunities to spend time with others? Are you isolating yourself because you're scared to reach out and become involved in the mainstream of life? Or are you forced by a physical condition to be alone much more than you wish? Whatever the reason, it is important to determine how much your emotions are getting in the way of a feeling of aloneness.

Often loneliness comes because of voluntarily staying in a situation long after it is good for you. The loneliness is only a symptom that something is wrong and you need to make some decisions about your life that honor your desire to be connected with people who are good for you. Your job then is to take charge of your life and *do* something about it.

YOU'VE GOT THE POWER

Look at your loneliness and decide what you want to do about it. It's only a state of mind.

☐ Own up to the feeling of loneliness and let others know of your condition. It is nothing to be ashamed about. But do not complain repeatedly about being alone: It is your job to reach out, take the first step, and then take steps to build connections with others.

☐ If you restrict yourself to only one kind of closeness, it will limit your opportunities to have a variety of emotional needs met. For example, you may want a close romantic relationship to fill your loneliness, so you exclude all relationships that do not fit that bill. Well, since you can't receive romance on command, you may spend many more lonely nights than if you open yourself to caring in a variety of ways for a variety of people.

☐ Be creative in the way in which you go about connecting with others. For example, let's suppose you are homebound because of a physical condition. You may ask others to come to you. Or you may use the telephone or a computer to connect with others, or you may decide to join a ham radio network and contact people all over the world. Although these ways carry constraints with them, you have as many opportunities to break through to others as you can devise.

WHAT TO DO AND SAY

▶ *Feeling shy, you do not take the first step in cultivating friends.*

Shy people are usually very self-conscious. Concentrating on how awkward *you* feel in a social situation often prevents you from really seeing the people around you. The next time you are invited out, concentrate on your surroundings. Really listen to the people around you and take an interest in what they say. Good listeners are very rare—and you'll be surprised at the interest *you* begin to generate.

The next step is to walk up to someone you would like to be friends with and say, "I'd like to get together in the coming week for lunch or a drink. Can you join me?"

You might also join a volunteer organization. You might be very surprised at what you personally get from your involvement with the project itself and from your fellow volunteers.

▶ *You are in a setting in which you do not naturally fit and in which others do not value who and what you stand for.*

If you find yourself in a group you cannot relate to, don't give up on groups in general—just *that* group. Ask yourself, "How did I get here? Am I doing something another person suggested I do or said I ought to do?" Your friend or relative may not have realized that the suggestion didn't fit you. Say, "Thanks for suggesting I join you, but this isn't for me." Teaching yourself to socialize is a process of fits and starts. Enjoy the process, and the odds are in your favor that with practice you will make your own circle of friends.

▶ *You think you are an awful person for being alone—but too awful to be with other people, too.*

Spending time alone is pretty awful when you don't like who you are. You may need to take a look at where and how you learned to dislike yourself. Were you abused? Did you live with someone who put you down or discounted you? Do you think you need counseling, or do you think you can work on your problems yourself?

Either way, start a program of positive affirmation, telling yourself, "I am lovable. I am likeable. I make a good friend. I am good to be with." Look into your mirror and practice smiling. Learn to be your own best friend. Experiment with ways to entertain yourself and begin to enjoy your time alone. Brighten up your surroundings—buy some new plants or paint your living room. Then invite some friends over for a meal. There is often an invisible barrier that interferes with starting projects. Once your self-help project is started, you may well get caught up in the activity, and once you begin to make friends with yourself, you'll find that it's much easier to make friends with others.

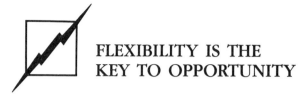

FLEXIBILITY IS THE KEY TO OPPORTUNITY

This is about rigidity. If you keep yourself focused on one path, one answer, and one angle, that is all you will see. The world will seem very limited because there are no other options other than the one you have settled on.

Fortunately, the world is really limitless. There are multitudes of ways to try to get what you want and millions of ways for it to present itself to you. But keep yourself open to possibilities. By seeing only one locked door, you could end up banging your head senseless because you didn't look six inches away to an open one. Maybe your one idea has worked well so far, but what if the end result could have been easier to achieve through other options?

Rigidity is learned and it can be unlearned. The key is in your flexibility. If you're willing to see the myriad avenues that are available to you, then they will appear. You'll vastly increase your chances of achieving what every healthy person wants: to meet their own needs.

YOU'VE GOT THE POWER

First, you have to let go of the belief that what you know or what you are doing is all there is.

☐ Tell yourself that a dead end is not a defeat of your goal. It may mean you need to try a different route or even another time.

☐ Open up your mind to other possibilities by finding out what they are.

WHAT TO DO AND SAY

▶ *You've been trying to get a job by reading the want ads. It's not working!*

With a career choice, read biographies, magazine articles, trade papers, journals, and how-to books on how others got into the field. Look for broadcast programs. Ask other people for their suggestions. Call someone in the business and say, "I respect you a great deal and know you're busy but I'm trying desperately to get into _____ and wondered if you could tell me how you did it and if you had any advice for me." When the traditional way doesn't work, get creative! See if you can take a lesser job in that field in order to get a foot in the door. Explore any idea you and your friends can come up with.

▶ *You and your partner want to move into a bigger house but can't afford it.*

For a new house, both of you could get second jobs or find better-paying ones. You could buy a fixer-upper and repair it yourself. If you don't have the skills, trade your talents with friends who do have them. Take in a boarder or a relative who could help with the mortgage. There are also lease-to-own options. Get some good advice from a realtor.

▶ *You want to make new friends but can't
    seem to find any who have your exact same
    interests.*

With friends, don't limit yourself to someone exactly
like you. The basics don't change even if your back-
grounds are different. See who feels good to you
instead of who looks and acts "just right," and make
that connection.

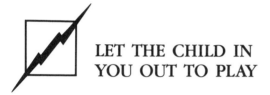

LET THE CHILD IN YOU OUT TO PLAY

Each of us has an inner child who wants to be loved,
protected, and played with. If you missed any of
these experiences when you were young, you will
want to recapture the elements as an adult. To the
degree to which your memories of childhood were
painful, your child part will reflect that pain now and
desire freedom from it.

The child part within provides us with fun and creativity. We cannot, however, access the creative, fun-
loving, spontaneous part without simultaneously
tapping into whatever else is stored nearby. It's like
opening Pandora's box: We get whatever is in there,
and we get all of it.

In psychological recovery from childhood pain, we
learn to heal ourselves. Often, however, once that job
is completed, we will find it necessary to give ourselves permission to learn *how* to express ourselves

playfully, to experience the delight that comes from smelling a flower or splashing in a warm spring rain.

Everyone does not experience fun the same way. It will be up to you to use your imagination while you experiment to find what you like and don't like. That's what childhood was supposed to be about. Having missed the opportunity for free expression may mean you'll need to watch others to see how they have fun.

YOU'VE GOT THE POWER

Give yourself permission to be the child you never were when you were small. Talk to the child part within you, saying, "Let's go have some fun today. It's time for you to learn to be a kid." Then do it.

WHAT TO DO AND SAY

▶   *You want to play more, but you don't know how.*

When you don't know how to have fun, watch children of all ages play and imitate them. With little kids, it may mean squishing your toes in the mud or doing creative dramatics. They experience the world in a sensory way—you can, too. You can drive the kind of car you wanted as a teenager, perhaps go for a ride in a hot-air balloon, build a sand castle on the beach, or learn to play tennis or bridge.

Try activities that you've never tried before. Use your imagination and release yourself from thinking there is a right or a wrong way to do whatever you want to do.

▶ *In the privacy of your home, you'd like to paint soap pictures on your chest as you luxuriate in the bathtub but you feel foolish and secretly worry that someone will find out.*

Feeling inhibited, even in privacy, means old programming is kicking into action and telling you not to have fun. Counter it by saying, "It's okay to be silly. I give myself permission. The grownup me is comfortable letting my kid out."

▶ *You spend weekends working very hard at your recreation rather than having fun, laughing, and kicking up your heels.*

Serious recreation isn't fun. The point of recreation is to have fun, not to be an expert. Although a few lessons can give you enough skill to have more fun, they can also begin to make what you are doing work. Choose partners who want to play at the same level you do.

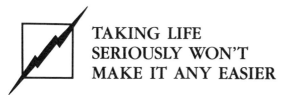

TAKING LIFE SERIOUSLY WON'T MAKE IT ANY EASIER

"Oh, grow up!"

"Would you act your age!"

"When are you going to start taking responsibility for yourself?"

It seems like the fun in life ends with childhood. Now you're supposed to be serious, act your age, avoid anything undignified. And you wonder why you're bored, frustrated, and want to be twelve again?

YOU'VE GOT THE POWER

The truth is you do need to take care of your responsibilities; it's how you go about it that makes the difference. Taking life very seriously will not make it any easier. But waking up each day deciding to find ways to have fun can. Quit taking yourself so seriously. Learn to laugh at your mistakes and celebrate your successes.

WHAT TO DO AND SAY

▶ *Every time you make a mistake, you chew yourself out.* ·

When you blow it, say to yourself, "Would you look at what I just did!" Then laugh about it. When you succeed, congratulate yourself.

▶ *You envy people who can relax and let their hair down.*

Being grown up doesn't mean you have to be miserable. Let the little child in you out to play. There are still parks to romp in, trees to climb, and balls to catch. Fingerpainting makes just as much a mess at forty-eight as at eight and clouds haven't lost their funny shapes. Look at life in terms of what amuses you—you'll find a lot of it will. Find people you can be silly with and enjoy their company—you'll find out how invigorating it can be.

▶   *You find yourself worrying about your children more than enjoying them.*

Tell yourself you're doing the best job you can as a parent. Give yourself permission to learn all you can about raising kids. Read books, attend parenting courses and talk to other parents. Then start appreciating the way being with your children allows you to express the child in yourself. Notice how they make everything fun. Children really "see" the world instead of just passing through it and you can see the wonder that you have become unaware of.

TAKE CARE OF
YOUR OWN
BUSINESS FIRST

Minding someone else's business means sticking your nose where it doesn't belong. It can be a thoughtless habit, but still needs to be unlearned for the comfort of all involved.

Sometimes there is a deeper meaning that serves a psychological purpose. The function is to act as a distraction from taking care of our responsibilities. When a marriage is in trouble, it's easier to try to tell grown kids how to raise their kids than deal with intimacy between you and your spouse. Criticizing someone else's job performance is easier than solving the basic problems of the company's structure. When you mind your own business, you will be so busy with your own life that there will be no time to mess with what others can do more effectively for themselves.

YOU'VE GOT THE POWER

When you find yourself minding someone else's business, ask yourself what it is accomplishing. What are you trying to avoid? Then, bite the bullet and take care of your own business.

WHAT TO DO AND SAY

▶ *An acquaintance asks whether you are pregnant yet—when you are struggling with infertility.*

If you are asked personal questions and feel you want an apology, say, "I feel uncomfortable that you asked the question. Did you mean to hurt me?" You may need to rebuild trust in the person if the relationship is to continue. Then say, "I don't want to talk about it."

▶ *Your officemate eavesdrops on your phone calls and tells you how to handle them.*

When your officemate eavesdrops, say, "I'd like to work in privacy. It distracts me to have someone looking over my shoulder." Then turn your back, talk more softly, or find another phone.

▸ *An activist spends hours protesting what other people choose to do with their free time rather than solving their own problems with closeness in their own family.*

When dealing with activists, say, "I'll handle my own business. I simply feel differently from you." There is no point in dialoguing with a person who *has* to mind another's business for psychological reasons. Trying to get him to face his own problems is not your business . . . and besides, it's impossible.

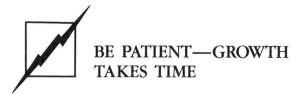

BE PATIENT—GROWTH TAKES TIME

Everything takes time to mature. If you impatiently push to get something done before it comes into its own time, you will weaken the foundation that supports the task or creation. This principle applies to projects as well as individuals. As children, we learn to walk when we're ready. No amount of practice with a 6-month-old is going to get those muscles walking sooner. Readiness is a matter of timing. When the time comes, you won't be able to hold yourself back.

It takes patience to allow a natural process to happen. But the rewards are sweet; just as sweet as the corn that is allowed to mature completely before picking.

YOU'VE GOT THE POWER

If you listen to your inner self, you know that you will mature at exactly the right time for you. Resist outside pressure. When you find that you are pressuring yourself, speak kindly but firmly to that authoritative voice within and reassure yourself that all will get done in time. Tell yourself, "Be patient. Growth takes time."

Projects come together when the elements that go into them are ready. Fretting and forcing may, in fact, create more glitches. When you factor other people into the project you will find a double dose of this maturation process at work. Keep working toward the goal, and keep your sense of humor.

WHAT TO DO AND SAY

> ▶ *You need a creative idea by the end of the week, but the more you try to think of one, the more blank your mind becomes.*

When creativity is involved, become clear about the end result you want to accomplish.

Talk with yourself, asking your intuition to go to work. Say, "I need an idea for this project. Please provide me with one. I trust you." Then completely let go of thinking of the project. What you are actually doing is giving the problem to your subconscious mind. This takes a leap of faith, but it works every time.

Watch for dreams, omens, and ideas that flow through your conscious awareness—usually at the moment you least expect it—in your bath, just as you wake up in the morning, even when you are thinking of something else. All of a sudden, your idea *will* come.

▶   *As an athlete, your coach presses you to be ready for a big meet, and during an extra workout you get injured.*

The next time someone tries to push you against your better judgment, you have learned that you have to be clear about your priorities. Say to your coach, "I want to give you what you want, but in the long run I'll be cheating you and the team if I push myself any harder. I'll take responsibility to do a great job in the game." A good coach will understand and use your skills to the team's best advantage. If he persists, then stand your ground. Say, "I can't give you what you want."

▶   *Your child wants to do things that older children are doing. He's not mature enough.*

Say, "I know you want to do that. Your time will come, but I'll help you wait until then." Find an activity, or form of expression, that is more fitting for the child's age.

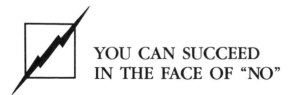

YOU CAN SUCCEED IN THE FACE OF "NO"

When someone says "No" to you, it does not mean you haven't any hope of getting what you wanted. You may have presented your idea at the wrong time, or you may have given it to the wrong person. You may even need to rethink it and come up with other alternatives.

It does not mean that you have to bang your head against the same unopenable door, or give up on the thought altogether and come up with something totally different.

You will want to see if the idea is still a good one, and review the original proposal for its merits and flaws. Then look for someone who can help you reframe your thoughts.

If it still offers the benefits you believed it would, start your presentation again. If not, let it go and come up with a new plan.

YOU'VE GOT THE POWER

When you get a "No," tell yourself not to panic. If you persevere, you will get what you need but maybe in a different way from what you originally planned.

WHAT TO DO AND SAY

▶   *A friend turns you down in your time of need.*

When you need help and are turned down, you could ask, "Are you uncomfortable with the whole request or just part of it? If I could break it down into pieces, or modify any request, or ask you again later, would you be willing to help me? If you still need to answer "no," it's okay with me." If the answer is still "no," look for someone else.

▶   *A boss says "No" to a request for a raise.*

Have your reasons ready when you request a raise. Keep the list in your head, because it might be easier for someone to discount the items if they're on paper. You could say, "I've reviewed my work. I've accomplished these goals, and I think an increase in my pay would help me work even more effectively."

If your boss thinks your work is poor, take an objective look and see if she's right.

If a tight budget is the problem, negotiate for something else you want: time off, a more flexible schedule, or a bigger desk.

If your boss is not open at all, tell yourself you're not trapped and that you will find a job that gives you what you want. Then quietly start looking for other options.

▶ *Someone says "I'm uncomfortable with that" to you.*

With "I'm uncomfortable," there is still room to bargain. Ask the person, "Is there anything I can do that would help you feel more comfortable with my request?" Then take it from there.

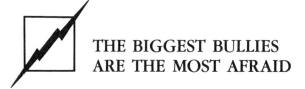

THE BIGGEST BULLIES ARE THE MOST AFRAID

It may be surprising that underneath the facade of a bully is a frightened person. Unable to cope with fear, the bully fools himself or herself by pretending to be bigger than life. A bully's actions are a dead giveaway. Don't be fooled by the surface image, the bravado, and the arrogance. Don't be afraid of what you see. You, with your awareness and acceptance of your fear, are more courageous than the bully.

Just remember that at some point, someone really picked on the bully. It probably happened in childhood and the perpetrator of abuse was no doubt bigger, stronger, and probably older. The bully became so afraid that he or she pushed the fear underground so it didn't have to be felt. To regain a feeling of power, the bully looked for smaller, younger, and weaker victims.

People with *real* talent, skill, and power don't go around bullying others, unless they initially were victims. People with real strength are often the most thoughtful of those who are weaker, and the most protective.

YOU'VE GOT THE POWER

When confronted with a bully be sure to protect yourself. Take a deep breath. Take a step back from the negative energy being sent out by the bully. Gather your inner strength and visualize the bully as a tiny, frightened child who is hurt.

☐ Be firm. A bully is looking for a willing victim. Do not respond to challenges presented by the bully and go about your business. If the bully is physically violent, of course, do what is necessary to protect yourself. Surround yourself with protective people and cease *any* contact with the person.

WHAT TO DO AND SAY

▶ *Your spouse bullies you, ranting and raving over every little thing you do or don't do.*

When any person, male or female, bullies you, remember that you don't deserve it. Say to your tormentor, "I don't deserve to be treated the way you are treating me. I realize that you feel differently from me, but you seem to be unaware of *my* feelings about this. If you don't like the way I do things, then do them to suit yourself."

You can only be dogged *if* you let it happen. Ask yourself how you were trained to accept unfair treatment, and realize that you need do so no longer. Tell yourself, "I'm okay. My ways are fine. I deserve to be treated well."

If your spouse threatens divorce, realize you don't have to be the one to file—let him or her do it. If the threat *is* only a threat, then suggest that you go to a marriage counselor to help you deal with your problems.

▶ *Your boss picks on the people he supervises, but kowtows to his boss.*

Bullies will use verbal threats to frighten their victims. If a boss repeatedly threatens to fire you, say, "If you feel that strongly about my work, then perhaps you need to fire me. But I think I'm doing a good job. I'd like for you to show me how you think I can improve." Ask for specifics, not generalities.

Know that the reason your boss ingratiates himself to his boss is the same reason he's a bully. As a child, he was abused by an authority figure. With his boss he plays the child role. With you, he plays the abusive authority role.

▶ *You notice that one of the players on your softball team often gets upset, scolding players who make errors.*

In team efforts, trying to work with a bully is tough. Members of the team can effectively confront the bully saying, "You're coming on a little strong— remember, it's just a game. We know that underneath you have many good qualities and we'd like to have you stay with us, but you need to tone it down. Are you willing to do that?" You have given the bully a chance to draw upon capabilities that have long been hidden within, and the chance to put aside the defensive behavior. You have shown your team mate that people who really care about him or her won't accept any bullying behavior.

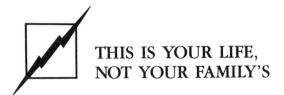

THIS IS YOUR LIFE, NOT YOUR FAMILY'S

Each family has its own attitudes, beliefs, and behaviors. Some are obvious and purposely chosen: These are the family traditions. Many others are unconsciously observed.

Written and unwritten rules can help groups stay together because the individuals feel that they have something in common. But you may never have felt comfortable with some of those rules and are still stuck unhappily following them. You do not have to be governed by anything your family does or believes.

Now that you are an adult and financially independent, you get to set your own standards and determine your own path. This is your life, not your family's. You may already have chosen to be emotionally healthier than they are. Now choose to make your day-to-day life one that you are happy to be living.

YOU'VE GOT THE POWER

Think about the things you feel you *have* to do with your extended family. Make a note to yourself whenever you feel uncomfortable about an activity with them. Remember you are acting for yourself, not against your family.

- ☐ Ask yourself: "What would I like to do instead?"

- ☐ Figure out how you can do it with your immediate loved ones or within the context of larger family events.

- ☐ Be tactful. You may want to start small and slow.

- ☐ Build up your confidence so that you won't seem belligerent when you choose to do something different.

WHAT TO DO AND SAY

▶   *Your family says you are "just like _____."*
      You don't want to be like that person but you
      are afraid they may be right.

Just because you are compared to a family member
does not mean you are or will be "just like" him or her,
even if you do look alike! You are a separate individual
who can make different and better choices than your
relative did. When you are compared, say, "I appreciate your concern but I feel good about my life and the
decisions I've made." Or if it's a real put-down, say,
"You're wrong. I don't want to talk about it anymore."
If you are told you're going to be just like another
relative who's more successful, say, "I appreciate the
compliment." Then let it go.

▶   *Your family defines itself by its cultural back-*
      ground. You don't like the restrictions that go
      along with that group.

You are not trapped by your heritage. If traditions are
keeping you from expressing your total self, create
some new ones. Remember, though, that you can
only change yourself, and your family may want to
stay the same. They may also want to pretend that
you are still the same. If they do ask, say, "I respect
your way but I'm happier doing it another way." If
you're told you ought to do something, say, "I think I
can make up my own mind about that," or say, "I've
decided to do something else that I think is better
for me."

▶ *Holidays are a big deal with your parents and siblings, but you want to have something quieter at home with just your spouse and kids.*

With holidays, there are a lot of options. You could spend the morning with your spouse and children and then have the big meal with everyone else. You could go every other holiday. You could have it at your house and invite everyone else to visit you.

You can also say, "No, we're not going because we're having a celebration at home with just our children this year. We want to start some traditions of our own."

If your family lives out of town, stay in a hotel so you can have some privacy.

 RESPECT YOURSELF

Respect has to do with self-esteem. You will experience self-respect when you value yourself. When your focus is on yourself, you don't worry about whether someone else is respecting you. Instead you communicate to others: "You are talking to a person who has self-respect." It is one of the greatest protections you can possibly acquire. Self-respect attracts respect from others like a magnet. You feel respect from another person because that person values what you do or how you act.

Do people have to *earn* respect? That depends. Neither parenthood, titles, nor age can truly *command* it. How you behave is the key factor. You cannot control whether you will be respected by someone else. You *can* control whether you respect yourself, and that is dependent upon your actions. Love yourself, live responsibly according to your beliefs, and you will experience the gift of self-respect. The rest will take care of itself.

YOU'VE GOT THE POWER

Have faith in yourself and your capacities. Work toward living a balanced life in a manner that is right for you. Balance is not attained by respecting others more than yourself, nor by respecting yourself more than other people. It comes from having esteem for both—and behaving that way.

☐ Tell yourself daily that you are a *good* person of equal value to those around you. Say, "I act and think in ways that I value. I respect myself." Match your behavior to your words.

☐ If you find that you demand respect, ask yourself "How am I lacking that I don't receive respect automatically?" Listen to your answers.

WHAT TO DO AND SAY

▶ *You've left your husband and you and your three-year-old have moved back to your parents' house until you can get on your feet.*

> *Your parents insist on treating you as a child,
> and your child is beginning to call your
> mother "mom."*

It is poisonous to your mental health to remain in an environment that does not treat you in a respectful way. It is important that you construct, or if necessary, seek an environment that is supportive of the true you. Keep control of your transition as much as you can.

▶ *You are very influenced by what others think
  of you and find it difficult to feel good about
  yourself when others ignore you. You are
  tempted to put your foot down to get the respect you deserve.*

Demanding the respect of others is only a distraction from facing your own lack of self-respect. When you are influenced by what others think, turn your attention back to you. Ask yourself how you lost your self-respect.

For example: "Was I put down as a child or pushed aside? Was I taught that other people matter more than I do? Did my parents have self-respect?" Realize as an adult that you can give yourself the respect you deserve. Then, you will automatically get it from others.

▶ *As a boss, you make a big show of leading a
  meeting with an iron hand. In reality you
  feel insecure and get very little done.*

It's important that you not substitute job power for personal self-respect. Use this opportunity to work on your self-respect so your inner worth can match your outer roles.

IT'S OKAY TO HAVE REQUIREMENTS OF OTHERS

It's hard not to have expectations of the people in your life, but your happiness can't depend on their living up to those hopes. You have no control over the actions of others. But you can decide how you feel about those actions.

You do want others to be honest with you and to treat you fairly, and those *are* requirements. They're appropriate because you know those qualities make you happy, and you want to surround yourself with people who have them.

Even so, no one will ever be able to do or say everything in exactly the way you want, because each of us is an individual. Even if someone else has the qualities you like, no one acts consistently in every situation or stays the same forever. People are human, and change is inevitable.

The key is to remember that your happiness does not depend solely upon the actions of others. When they can't live up to your expectations, don't fall apart. Because you *can* always meet your own needs. Then enjoy the person for what he does have to give you.

YOU'VE GOT THE POWER

Make a list of what you require in other people.

☐ Decide if the people in your life fulfill those requirements and to what degree.

☐ If they don't, you have to make a decision.
"Am I going to accept them as they are, or do
I need to let them go?"

With expectations, you have more leeway. Make a
list of what you would like to see in others.

☐ Some people may have only a few of those
characteristics; others, more. Decide if the
former are still worth keeping around.

☐ Then realize that no one can give you 100%
every time.

☐ Know that you can always count on yourself.

WHAT TO DO AND SAY

▶ *You require your partner to hold up his end
of the relationship financially.*

A relationship is a partnership in which each party
needs to contribute. It is appropriate for you to require your partner's financial input. It is also common for partners to trade supporting one another
monetarily while the other works to achieve his
goals and those of the relationship. If you are the
only one working, then you may need to discuss
what he intends to do to hold up his financial responsibilities. If your partner has been disabled, you
can contact the various federal and local agencies
that can provide support. If he is able and unwilling
to work and your discussions have not made a difference, you may need to consider counseling. If you
continue to be taken advantage of, then you may
need to end the relationship.

▶ *You expect your boss always to be friendly to you. When she gets distant, you panic because you think you're going to lose your job.*

If your boss doesn't act friendly, it may have nothing to do with you. She may be busy thinking about something else and not notice you. In fact, your need to be recognized could be a major distraction. If you're concerned about your job, evaluate your own performance. If you would like to discuss how you can improve, make an appointment to talk with your boss. If that's not possible, meet with someone you work with, or someone from outside your company, to get a different perspective. Take care of your insecurity first before it creates a problem that doesn't exist.

▶ *You invite a close friend to your party and she doesn't show up.*

Just because you're there for someone else all the time doesn't mean she can be there for you. Your friends can only do the best they can at any given moment. Remind yourself of the times that person has been a good friend. Then say, "Hey, I missed you at the party last night! Is everything okay?"

If your friend is the kind of person who chronically makes plans and then lets you down, ask, "Are you aware that whenever we make plans, you find a reason to cancel?" Sometimes calling attention to a problem can stop it. If not, then quit making arrangements that you know aren't going to work out.

BUSINESS AND PLEASURE DON'T ALWAYS MIX

You'll meet a lot of people on the job or through networking with whom you may have great working relationships. But it doesn't necessarily mean that you'll be friends with them.

YOU'VE GOT THE POWER

Some people want to keep a definite line between work and play. Some may only be able to think of you as a colleague and not a buddy. Also, characteristics that have made them successful in their careers may make them lousy friends.

Likewise, you may have great friends who you would trust with your life, but you cannot do business with them. Their laid-back attitude may be fine in your backyard, but you need a tiger in the office. Or their demand to win may be great on the tennis court, but could threaten your ability to solve problems in a company setting.

WHAT TO DO AND SAY

▶   *A friend who is also a colleague has just become the new manager. Because of his insecurity, a little power has turned him into a tyrant.*

Power can do strange things to insecure people. Some may be unable to make any decisions. Others are so afraid of making a mistake that they try to control and manipulate everyone and everything so that they won't be blamed. They may want the job so badly that they'll do anything to keep it—including hurting the people around them.

Your new boss may be tougher on you because he doesn't want anyone to accuse him of playing favorites. So don't rely on your friendship to get you understanding—that may be what's causing the problem in the first place. Approach him as you would any boss. You can even say, "I leave our friendship at the door when I come in here." You may lose a friendship, or it may return when he gains more self-confidence. Just don't hold your breath.

▶ *You work with someone you'd like to be*
   friends with, but she turns down all of your
   invitations.

When you want to know someone better, ask the person directly, "I really enjoy working with you and would like to get to know you better. Would you be comfortable going out to lunch on Saturday?" If not, let it go and look for someone else.

▶ *Your best buddy wants to go into business*
   with you. You aren't sure how you'd work to-
   gether.

When you want to go into business with a friend, know that it's rare to find someone with whom you can work and play, but it can happen. Ask yourself:

What qualities does he or she have that would help us succeed?

What qualities make me uncomfortable when I picture us in the work place?

How good are we at negotiating? Would we be able to work out problems without getting mired in a power struggle?

How well-defined are my own boundaries? Do I allow my friend to run my life all the time?

Remember, too, that whenever there is a threat of losing money and power, a person's fears about those issues could make him controlling, argumentative, and hard to reason with. Talk about how each of you will take care of your own needs in the bad times and good.

If you decide to go into partnership, realize that your business relationship may not be as easy as your friendship has been. Be committed to solving the problems that do occur. Plan out exactly what you want to accomplish; what each partner's role will be; how you'll arrive at final decisions; where the money will go, and for what; and what you'll do if it doesn't work out. Treat this like a marriage: It's not what you do know but what you don't that can make you miserable down the road.

If you decide that a business relationship wouldn't work, say, "I'm more comfortable with just being friends," or "I'm afraid we'd jeopardize our friendship if we ran into a situation we couldn't handle."

IT'S THE INTENT BEHIND THE WORDS THAT MATTERS

If you've ever had the experience of being repeatedly hurt or sabotaged by someone who then says a phrase such as, "I'm sorry," you no doubt know that the conciliatory phrase doesn't make you feel any better. Any time a person uses words that are not followed by a change in behavior, he either doesn't plan to change or is unable to change. The words are being used as a smoke-screen. They free the speaker to continue behaving in the old way.

The failure to match words and behavior begins in childhood when truth is discouraged. Granted, parents don't intend to teach kids to lie, but nonetheless, it happens. Little children are taught to say, "I'm sorry," any time they do something that isn't acceptable behavior. In reality they are not truly sorry. Children act this way because they are trying to meet their needs and they have learned quickly that they are off the hook if they just say, "I'm sorry" after an offense. Instead, children need to be taught that the statement needs to be saved for true accidents that were not intended.

For similar reasons, older children may say quickly "just kidding" after making an offensive remark. In this way they can express negative feelings to someone they do not want to directly confront. If the pattern continues, they have learned to lie about their real feelings and to build themselves up at the expense of others.

Other variations include the phrases, "I understand," "I know how you feel," and "I know." The motive behind "I understand" is often to bridge differences. The motive behind "I know how you feel" is often to avoid uncomfortable feelings. The motive behind "I know" is often to get people off our backs.

The habits adults learn as children do not miraculously go away, and when habits become ingrained the behavior becomes automatic. Any time a behavior repeats more than a time or two, followed by one of the phrases, you know to look for something deeper. The words act as an excuse to continue the behavior without changing.

YOU'VE GOT THE POWER

"I'm sorry," of course, is acceptable when an accident occurs.

But don't put a lot of emphasis on accepting the apology alone. When a person admits their fallibility in a situation and follows up by taking the responsibility to overcome their frailty, then say, "I know you are working to correct the situation and I support you." If the pattern recurs, however, you may want to discuss the differences you see between the words and behavior.

WHAT TO DO AND SAY

▶   *Your spouse is chronically late getting ready to go out, but always says "I'm sorry" as if*

*that eliminates the responsibility to do any-
thing about the lateness.*

If your spouse continues to repeat the offending behavior (being late), it is important to jump over the
apology or phrase and ask what his plans are to
change the behavior. Then respond, "I hear you say,
'I'm sorry' but it doesn't seem to be helping you
solve the problem of being late. Do you know why
you are doing this? If I can help you with it, let me
know. Otherwise I need to go on ahead and you can
follow when you are ready." You can then take two
cars, or your spouse can call a taxi.

▶   *A friend is grieving and you wonder whether
      saying, "I understand how you feel," is the
      right thing.*

Never say "I understand" to someone in grief. That is
a time to say, "I'm sorry," and that's all that can be
said.

▶   *An employee continues to gossip after being
      told not to. When you confront the person
      you hear, "I know, I know."*

On the job, you need to clearly state your limits: "I
leave the responsibility for your behavior with you.
If I hear of this happening one more time, I'll have
to reassign you or let you go." This leaves the responsibility with the other person. You must be firm and
serious with someone who makes light of trying to
change.

▶ *You tell your friend that you are tired of being let down when she doesn't follow through on her promises. She says, "I understand," but you have the feeling that you can't trust her.*

With a friend who continues to let you down, say, "No, thank you," if the person offers again. If pressed, say, "I can't take the risk of being let down." Don't ask that person for help. You're just setting yourself up for trouble.

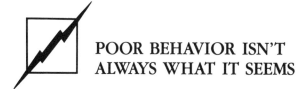

POOR BEHAVIOR ISN'T ALWAYS WHAT IT SEEMS

If you love mysteries then you'll love figuring out the reasons behind poor behavior. Whether it is in you or someone else, behavior that is hurtful, inadequate, or destructive is always a cover-up. There is another story underneath that is just not apparent on the surface. This behavior is a symptom that there is a pain inside, and in order to get rid of it, the person is trying to transfer the pain to somebody else.

Let's suppose you denigrate another person. A verbal attack is destructive behavior that may indicate the presence of jealousy. *Why* are you jealous? Jealousy is always a symptom of poor self-esteem and feelings of inadequacy. This may be the real culprit behind the problem behavior, and this is the problem that should be addressed. As temperature indicates the health of our bodies, behavior indicates the health of our emotions.

YOU'VE GOT THE POWER

When someone behaves poorly toward you, "turning the other cheek" or otherwise ignoring the slight shows that you accept that behavior and allows that behavior to continue. Because *you* don't want to feel unnecessary pain, it is your responsibility to ensure that the behavior won't recur.

For this reason, discuss the behavior when it happens. Some people will be honest and share their real feelings. Others will say they don't understand and may even attack by telling you you are making a mountain out of a molehill. The fact is, they probably *don't* understand what really drove them to behave poorly, and if this is the case, there is little you can do other than set firm limits on their future behavior. Say, "I'm unwilling to let you abuse me. If you do, I'll have to leave." You can't solve their real problem but you can protect yourself from being hurt by it.

When you find that you have behaved badly, look into yourself and try to discover the real reasons why. Then satisfy the needs that are causing your poor behavior.

WHAT TO DO AND SAY

▶   *Your partner accuses you of not caring about him anymore and throws a tantrum.*

Say to your partner, "I am trying to understand *why* you are acting the way you are. The problem is, your temper tantrum doesn't tell me what you are feeling inside. All I hear is the anger. I'd like to listen to your words." Then, wait and see what he is able to do. The problem may be that your spouse feels that you are not giving him enough attention. By giving him attention now, and listening to what he has to say, you may prevent further outbursts. If your spouse is not capable of reasonable discussion, then say, "I care about your pain, but I am unwilling to be around you when you are having a temper tantrum. Let me know when you are through. Then I'd like to try to help." Leave immediately.

▶ *A coworker isn't sharing fully in the workload, yet accuses the rest of you of taking advantage of her.*

On the job, you may need to point out to your colleague that her behavior does not fit the current situation. Ask the person, "Why do you seem to feel you are being taken advantage of? I don't see it. Specifically, what am I doing?" Then listen to what the person has to say. Be empathetic but realistic as you discuss the situation. Say, "I know you have value and that you will hold up your end of the job. I will hold up mine and let me know if you feel I've let you down."

▶ *Your four-year-old clings to you, whining and needing a lot of extra attention.*

When a child develops behavior that is offensive, invariably that is the only way the child has to communicate some other problem. For example, a youngster who has been badly frightened is likely to whine and cling but can't say, "I'm scared because I don't like to be left alone when you go out or so and so abused me." You, however, can play detective and say, "Something must be hurting you. You can tell me. There are no secrets between you and me. I'll listen because I love you and want to protect you and make you happy. But I don't know what you need when you whine. Use a regular voice to tell me what you need."

YOU CAN BENEFIT FROM WHAT YOU DON'T UNDERSTAND

Events will occur in your life that you won't have any explanation for or any control over. You can either be threatened by them or pretend they don't happen, or you can use them to help you achieve what you thought was unattainable.

Some people call it luck, or chance, or fate, but it does exist and it's a wonderful way for you to build your power. You can wake up every day with the thought that anything, no matter how far-fetched, could happen. You might not understand it but it could still happen. With that idea in your head throughout every day, how could you not be happy?

YOU'VE GOT THE POWER

Take the pressure off yourself by deciding to let things happen instead of trying to force them.

☐   Be aware of your surroundings so that you'll know when unexplainable events are going on and can appreciate them.

☐   Accept the unexplainable as completely normal and it will become so.

WHAT TO DO AND SAY

▶   *You think about a person you haven't seen in years and then run into her in a store.*

When you run into someone you haven't seen in awhile, say, "I was just thinking about how great it would be to see you, but I didn't know where to find you!" Ask yourself, "Is there any particular reason why I wanted to see this person at this moment?"

▶   *A job opportunity that you never believed you could be qualified for is offered to you out of the blue.*

Expand your mind when it comes to your own abilities. Instead of limiting yourself to the job you are doing at the moment, say, "I can do anything I put my mind to." Then be open to any kind of opportunity that comes your way. You don't have to say "Yes" to all of them. Check out your feelings first. Some of them may just be compliments to your open-mindedness.

▶ *Your intuition often guides you in difficult situations, but you aren't sure whether to trust it.*

If you're avoiding a lot of everyday hassles, you're probably listening to your intuition or inner voice. Your life doesn't have to be full of problems for you to learn what you want to know. Let what is often the smartest part of you tell you where to go, what to do, and who to do it with. It can help you set up a smooth rhythm in your life that will keep you happy and focused.

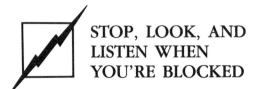

STOP, LOOK, AND LISTEN WHEN YOU'RE BLOCKED

You know the feeling of being blocked, from a goal or the fulfillment of a desire or a wish. No matter how hard you try, you can't seem to break through the barrier to your success. You may be frustrated but there is a reason for the block being there. Some-times it is because you are trying to do something that really is not in your best interest. Or you may be trying to do something counter to the expectations of others. It could be trying to guide you to follow a feeling. At other times, the block or blocks are there as a function of timing; i.e., the society/workplace or relationship is not ready for whatever it is that you want to do.

We are the only instrument we have in order to achieve in life: The achievement of our goals is dependent on us for accomplishment. If we are out of order then there is little likelihood we will reach our goals. We may lack the courage to accomplish what we dream about doing. Or we may have unfinished psychological business to attend to before we go further in our achievements. It is common to experience blocking at these times. It is up to us to do whatever needs to be done in order to become a fully functioning person . . . an instrument that is in good shape.

Regardless of the reasons for the blocks, they are always there to serve some purpose. We need to seek that purpose rather than trying to force our way past the block. The result is always twofold: to release the block and to help ourselves in some way to reach our goals.

YOU'VE GOT THE POWER

When you become aware that things are not moving smoothly for you, look for the block. As you look for the block you may hit on some aspect that causes you discomfort. The pain signifies that you are getting to the cause and the block, so ask yourself why you feel so uncomfortable.

☐ Don't *try* to think up the answer. Let the answer come to you.

☐ If you are blocked and people want to know why, say, "I'm working on figuring that out. If you have any ideas, I'm open to hearing them." Asking for support will relieve you of some of the tension you feel. Tension can make blockages worse.

☐ Set the problem aside for a few days to give yourself a break. Often we can work blocks out if we just let go of them on the conscious level for the time being.

WHAT TO DO AND SAY

▶   *You are expecting a child and you and your spouse are trying to buy a house. You lost the last one because someone made a better offer, and there are problems with contract negotiations on this one.*

The pressure to "make a nest" before the baby comes may be clouding your judgment. Say to your spouse, "I don't know why we are not succeeding in getting a contract to go through, but I don't like the feeling of pressure that we are under now. I don't think it's a good time to make our move. Let's delay six months and then see about moving *after* the baby is born." The timing may simply be wrong, and that's why it doesn't come easy. Let it go for the moment.

▶   *You are in a relationship that doesn't seem to be working. Nothing is really wrong, but nothing is really right, either. There seems to be a wall between you.*

When you and your special friend hit a luke-warm period in your relationship, acknowledge the feelings to yourself. Let some time go by, days or even a few weeks. If the feelings don't go away, say to your friend, "I've noticed a difference in our friendship, have you? Let's talk." It may be a sign of poor communication. Or it could be that the relationship has run it's course. Be honest with what you are feeling. Trust your feelings to figure out what the block is in your relationship and honor the outcome.

▶ *You have a creative idea but are thwarted in all your attempts to find an outlet.*

Stop and ask yourself, "What might be the function of this block? How can I constructively use the time to improve myself and my skills until a breakthrough happens?" It is not unusual to experience slowdowns and disappointments when we need to gain additional skills in order to be more effective when we do become successful. The trick is how to use the time productively, until an opportunity arises.

Rely on trusted friends for support while you explore adjacent avenues of interest. Sometimes the answer to a problem comes in unexpected ways. You may need to develop a plan of attack to move your creative ideas out into the world. A specialist in the field of marketing, distribution or sales may be useful at this point.

Know and believe that every creative idea has value. It's just that the timing may be different from what you would like or expect. Believe in yourself and persevere.

IF YOU CAN'T CLIMB OVER THE MOUNTAIN, WALK AROUND IT

Sometimes the path to our goals is obstructed by obstacles that are bigger than our ability or power to remove them.

It is, however, not necessary to give up our goal entirely. Nor is it necessary to bloody ourselves to try to break through the obstacle. Persevering at all cost is not always the smartest thing to do. Instead it may be quite possible to achieve the goal by taking a detour. Sure the path may be longer or look less beautiful but if it gets us there, why not?

YOU'VE GOT THE POWER

Sometimes power lies in knowing your own limits, and this requires no apology. Be realistic about your capabilities, and if you cannot reach a goal in one way, then approach it from another direction.

Know the reasons behind your behavior. You don't need to share them. They're for your private use.

WHAT TO DO AND SAY

▶   *You have a coworker who undermines you by openly countermanding directions you give to your joint-support staff. You do not feel strong enough to confront the person openly.*

If you don't have the emotional or job power to face down a coworker, engage in a little environmental manipulation. One solution is to split the support staff between the two of you. Suggest that your colleague meet separately with part of the group to accomplish a special project. Say, "I know you can do an exceptional job with this special project and I'll cover the bases with what's left."

If the separation plan doesn't work, go to your boss saying, "I need your help." Be objective and simply state what happened when you were undermined but don't label it as undermining. Ask for advice.

▶ *Your new job in human relations requires you to give a presentation to the 200 executives in your company on new policies. You feel overwhelmed.*

When any new activity frightens you, break it up into small pieces. Set your limits by arranging to talk to only fifteen people at a time. Know your material backwards and forwards. Realize that what interests your audience most is not you personally, but what you have to tell them. Practice, practice, practice. After your first meeting, it will get easier.

▶ *Your son asks you to take care of your three grandchildren for a week while your daughter-in-law accompanies him on an out-of-town conference. You love your grandchildren but you know you can't cope with them for a week.*

To your son say, "I wish I could take care of the children but I'm not up to it. I'd like to help out, but I can't handle them for that long. Let me help you brainstorm other options." It's okay to be firm and if your son gets offended, he's frustrated. Say, "I know you are frustrated. I also know you will find a solution." You might offer to take them for some of the time.

It's okay to refuse to take on more than you are comfortable handling. It doesn't matter if someone else can handle three kids. If it feels too much for you, then don't do it.

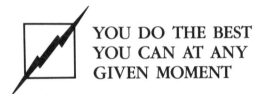

YOU DO THE BEST YOU CAN AT ANY GIVEN MOMENT

We all do the best we can at any given moment. When we make a decision, we weigh all the information available to us and we choose what seems to be the best possible option. Depending on the situation, the decision-making process can take a split-second or several months.

Hindsight makes each of us aware of all kinds of information and results that were not available at the time we took an action or made a decision. If the decision turned out to be successful, hindsight allows us to congratulate ourselves on our wisdom. But if the decision had negative repercussions, we use hindsight to criticize ourselves, tear our hair, or in other ways berate ourselves for having chosen the option we chose. We may even remember an alternative that, as time has shown, would have been better.

But it is useless to punish ourselves over paths we have already taken. To say we should have had more courage, or ought to have chosen X over Y, changes nothing. If we had had the courage, we would have used it. If Y seriously looked like the better option, we would have chosen it. We made the best decision we could at the time, and instead of using hindsight to punish ourselves, it is more productive to use it as a learning experience.

YOU'VE GOT THE POWER

Give yourself the credit you deserve: You truly did the best you possibly could at the time.

- [ ] Forgive yourself for being self-critical about the choices you made.

- [ ] Separate yourself from the criticisms of others who cannot know the full story behind your decision. You can do this by being honest with them and yourself. Say to the critic, "I realize I hurt you. I am sorry. I did the best I could then, and I'm doing the best I can now." Then reaffirm to yourself, saying, "I am doing the best I can."

- [ ] Look at your behavior, then consider other options that you might have taken. Run through the new scenario in your head seeing a more constructive outcome.

☐ Affirm to yourself that you have learned from your experience and that if a similar situation arises again, this new knowledge will give you better judgment. Say, "I can think clearly about every situation I'm in. I have options. I am a capable, responsible person, and I do the best I can do at any given moment."

WHAT TO DO AND SAY

▶ *You reacted to an emergency by freezing on the spot.*

If you froze in an emergency, forgive yourself and then practice reacting to emergencies. Role-playing would help. Say, "I can think clearly in an emergency situation," and visualize yourself doing this.

▶ *You tried to keep a burglar from taking your purse and ended up getting mugged.*

Reconstruct the mugging situation in your mind after you talked with the police about safety tips. You may even decide to take a course in self-defense. Give yourself permission to let your belongings go. Say, "My safety is more important than my belongings."

▶ *You yelled at your boss and quit after he berated you in front of your coworkers.*

Begin to work on your temper. Any time you get even a little angry, stop as soon as you become aware of it and think of other alternatives to get what you want. You'll begin to break the cycle of getting out of control. Say to yourself, "I'll find out why I got so angry and I'll fix it in myself. I won't lose my job again because I lose control."

▶   *You love your kids a lot and tried to raise them to be self-controlled and successful. You find out later that they resent many of the things you did.*

It's a good idea to sit down with adult children and say, "I did the best I knew how at the time. I loved you and still do and always wanted everything for you. I see now that I made mistakes. I'm willing to hear your angry feelings and resentment from the past, but I also want to get past them. I ask you to forgive me. I'm willing to help you correct the mistakes I made."

If one of your children is not ready to forgive you yet, just back off for now. And above all, forgive yourself.

TRANSITIONS CAN BE SURVIVED

We tend to live our lives in chapters. When we're snugly nestled into a chapter, we feel stabilized. But if we are to grow, chapters must come to an end—otherwise we get stuck in a rut. The period of time between the chapters is a time of transition, fraught with insecurity and fears of the unknown. It is the time of change and it has a different set of characteristics than the stable chapters have.

Even when we initiate change ourselves, we find that there is always a point where we meet the unknown. It is usually at the moment that we let go of the past but have not yet discovered the future. If you're feeling afraid, it may help to know that the feelings we are having are absolutely normal.

It is also normal to feel a sense of loss about the old even when the past was unpleasant or is no longer desirable. But there is also a sense of anticipation and delight in the new mingled with fear about what is not yet within the realm of our experience. That is what makes life fun.

As soon as we open a new door, we start developing new patterns and habits of security. It is only a matter of taking a deep breath and bridging the unknown until it begins to feel familiar.

YOU'VE GOT THE POWER

Tell yourself this won't last forever. Then say "I am leaving an old chapter. I am in transition. It will only take a while until I get used to the new chapter in my life."

☐ Transitions are also made easier if you trust in some Higher Power. Because you are in uncharted territory, it helps to believe you will be protected in your passage and that ultimately the outcome will be positive for you.

☐ It's a good idea, at such times, to ask for support. You can say, "I could use a good friend at a time like this." It's especially useful to seek out someone whose been down the road ahead of you. Say, "I am in transition and would appreciate your support."

☐ It's a nice gesture to offer support to someone going through a transition; you can say, "I know, I've been there and you'll make it. I trust in you."

WHAT TO DO AND SAY

▶ *You are beginning something new (you get married; have a baby; graduate from school; move to a new city; get divorced; retire) and you're wondering if you can handle it.*

In any new situation, it's important to give yourself six months to a year getting adjusted. Be very patient with yourself, as you learn to play new roles. It helps to establish a regular routine. Nurturing also helps. Pull out old-time favorite ways you've taken care of yourself and see whether they will work. (They probably will.)

▶ *A special relationship moves to another layer of intimacy and vulnerability, and you are feeling very insecure.*

Intimate relationships take careful handling, especially when we move from one layer of intimacy to another. Each transition brings out our deepest fears, yet out greatest strengths. Be honest, trustworthy, and sensitive to your partner. Be sure to tell your partner, "I'm scared too. But we'll make it. I love you."

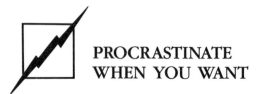

PROCRASTINATE WHEN YOU WANT

You know your trouble is procrastination when you say:

> "I'm going to . . . when I . . ."
> "I ought to get started . . ."
> "I shouldn't have left it till the last minute."

Obviously, none of these statements has action attached to it. Each is a wish, hope, or expectation that is left dangling without an anchor attached. Each represents a job that is incomplete or judged to have been done in an unacceptable manner.

The problem is, however, that it is impossible to tell the reasons behind the procrastination. Some of those reasons may even be sound, belying the bad reputation that procrastination has. You may be trying to do something that you feel you should do but don't really want to do. In that case, your procrastination is trying to get you to be true to yourself, even though you may have been taught that leaving something until the last minute was bad. Or you may procrastinate because you are one of those people who does best by giving a project your all at once, after having let the idea simmer for a long time. It's also possible that you procrastinate because you are not ready to undertake a task. Procrastination is saving you from getting in over your head. Each of these reasons for waiting to do something is valid and in your best interest.

Granted, sometimes procrastination is a symptom that you will want to work to change. It could be the result of fear learned as a child because you were scolded about the quality of your workmanship. Or perhaps you had a perfectionistic parent or teacher whose standards you observed and could never meet. There may even be a fear of completing a project that keeps you from starting it.

It's important to figure out what the delays in your action represent. Don't judge yourself until you do this. When others call you a procrastinator, you must stop and evaluate what they mean. Then take charge of your behavior and procrastinate when it serves your purposes.

YOU'VE GOT THE POWER

Analyze *why* you are putting off starting or completing that project. Then give yourself permission to:

☐ Start slowly

☐ Develop your own work style

☐ Do only what you want to do

☐ Develop at your own pace

☐ Do a good job

☐ Enjoy all the small things you accomplish.

☐ Tell anyone who questions your work patterns that you prefer to work your own way and will take responsibility for getting it done on time.

WHAT TO SAY AND DO

▶   *Your parents want you to buy a house near them. You keep putting off meeting with a realtor.*

When anyone tries to get you to do something you really don't want to do, it's time to be honest. Say, "I realize I have been putting off talking with a realtor, but I've discovered I like the other side of town better. We'll still see you often, though."

▶   *You have a project deadline but don't seem to be able to get going because, once you start, you know it will consume your whole life as you try to make it perfect.*

When you tend to be a perfectionist, say to yourself, "It's okay to do a less than perfect job. I'll enjoy the work as you do it rather than looking for the "grade" at the end." You may even want to set a limit on how much time each day you allow yourself to work on the project. Then assign yourself play time after that.

Beware of calling yourself a perfectionist. Having heard yourself labeled that many times, you may have come to believe it. Then, each time you have a project to complete, you forewarn everyone around, teaching them you are a perfectionist. Stop! Zip up your mouth and use whatever timing you wish to finish the job.

▶ *You keep delaying a return to school because you are afraid you'll fail.*

When you delay a return to school because you're afraid you'll fail, start small. Take one course. Be sure to visit the counseling center to ask for help and let friends support you. Most important of all, do not become a hermit, hiding what you are doing from others. Let them help you. Go for it!

STICK TO IT AND YOU'LL DO IT

Perseverance sounds like one of those old-fashioned words like diligence and duty that doesn't have anything to do with today's world. Yet it is the key to meeting your goals.

YOU'VE GOT THE POWER

Who you know may sometimes be more important than what you know, but what really matters is how long you're willing to hang in there until your dream comes true.

Don't hesitate, or give yourself time to think of reasons not to do it. DO IT! The next thing you know, you'll be writing a book or singlehandedly fixing the car. Once you've done something you didn't know you could, you may start thinking about other dreams that you thought were beyond you and mastering those, too.

WHAT TO DO AND SAY

▶   *You want to be successful in a certain career. It always seems just out of reach and you're about to give up.*

For most people, success in a career is a matter of timing and readiness. First ask yourself: "Does this career choice fit me?" If it does, tell yourself: "This is what I love to do and I will achieve what I want when I'm ready for it."

Meanwhile, spend the time mastering your craft so that when your opportunity arrives—and it will— you'll be prepared to handle the rewards and to excel in your field.

▶   *You're trying to finish a college degree part-time and it's taking years. You're wondering if it's worth it.*

With any kind of schooling, there is no age limit on learning. What you pick up in college will help you in all kinds of areas and always in the job market. What's important is that you're not obsessed about how long it's taking or what year you'll finish. Be sure to make time to play and fulfill yourself as an emotionally healthy person, not just a career-minded individual. If you need a break, take it. Then get back on track.

▶ *You're learning to do something new. It seems way too hard and that you'll never understand it.*

When you're trying to learn anything new, don't let your feelings stop you from expanding your abilities. When you're frustrated, let it out and then tell yourself: "This is not that hard. I can do it and I will give myself the time I need. I'll also use my creativity to see if I can find easier ways to achieve my goal."

BE PROUD OF YOURSELF

Being proud of yourself is quite different from having pride that can get in your way. It's also different from the pride one person feels in another's achievements. When you are proud of something you do, you take responsibility for both the achievement and the work you put into the activity. It's important to do that so you can reinforce your capability and self-esteem. Similarly, all kinds of growth—educational, psychological, and spiritual—take work. Be proud of your accomplishments in these difficult areas.

Be careful about false pride, however. Being too proud to ask for help is due to a belief that you don't deserve the help or that you *should* be able to take care of yourself. Both are learned beliefs. Neither fits our humanness. Since there are no superhumans, everyone needs help at one time or another. You deserve all the help you can get. Your job is to make good use of the help.

Having someone take pride in what you do is a bit like robbery. It takes responsibility for your achievement away from you. Parents have a great tendency to do this. Children, in turn, tend to achieve *for* their parents' approval. No one wins in this scenario.

When you work for your own self and enjoy those achievements, everyone comes out a winner. Pat yourself on the back, know your limits and make compensations for them. Be proud of who and what you are because there is no one finer.

YOU'VE GOT THE POWER

Make a list of your achievements.

- ☐ Acknowledge each achievement.

- ☐ Review what it took to reach your goals.

- ☐ Tell yourself that you are proud of what you have done.

- ☐ Say "Thank you" to the hard working, persistent part of you that achieved that goal for you.

- ☐ Tell one person of your accomplishments.

- ☐ Celebrate together.

WHAT TO DO AND SAY

▶ *You worked very hard to get your behavior under control after learning many nonfunctional lessons in childhood. You deserve to feel good about what you have done.*

Tell yourself what a good job you have done with your emotions and behavior, turning a dysfunctional person—you—into an emotionally healthy, coping human being. Say, "I'm proud of me for the work I've done. It's not always been easy, but I never quit. I've got guts and I deserve a big pat on the back."

▶ *You lost your job but have too much pride to let people know, so you find yourself having a lot of trouble making contacts for another job.*

There is no shame in having lost a job. Say to yourself, "I did the best I could do. Now I need to do the best I can to find a new job. That means being honest and open with the fact that I am out of work so I can network with other people."

When that little voice inside says, "You shouldn't have to ask for help," ask yourself where you learned that. It is a false belief that creates false pride. Tell the little voice, "Thank you for trying to help me feel strong and good about myself, but I have a new and better way, so I dismiss you now."

Then, show *real* courage and begin to network with people who know what jobs are available and how to get them. Good luck!

▶ *You feel uncomfortable when your parents point to you, declaring loudly to all who will listen that you are a professional person of whom they are enormously proud.*

Realize when your parents puff up over your accomplishments that they may be trying to live through you. Sometimes parents are insecure about their parenting and need to look at you for reassurance they did a good job. Or they feel inadequate about themselves and need to feel better by taking pride in you.

Though they don't mean to harm you, you may wish to temper their intrusion into your life. You can say to them, "It makes me uncomfortable when you speak about me in public. Please don't do it." If they argue with you or say you are too sensitive, just repeat, "It makes me uncomfortable and I'm asking you not to do it any longer." If your parents are an especially tough case, you may want to say, "Stop, or I'll have to walk away." You can train them to keep a lower profile even if you can't get them to cease living through you.

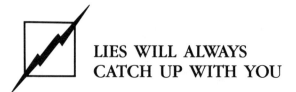

LIES WILL ALWAYS CATCH UP WITH YOU

People lie for many different reasons. Some see lying as a stretching of the truth that won't hurt anyone. Others want to embroider their part in a story to make themselves seem larger than life. Then it just becomes a habit.

Some people lie but don't know they are doing it. They honestly believe that what they are saying will come true even if it has no basis in fact. Fear can cause people to lie because they want to be liked so badly that they will pretend to be what you want in order to gain your acceptance. There are pathological liars who can't control themselves. But they are a small percentage.

Why do people lie? Maybe because it's easy. Most people will take what you say at face value. And sometimes it's hard to tell the difference between a lie and reality because you think what you tell yourself *is* the truth. That's why positive thinking, taping new messages, and saying affirmations work so well.

Lies are almost always a cover-up for fear or low self-esteem. They may make you feel good for the moment, but you'll feel worse later when they catch up with you. It's almost impossible to consistently tell everyone the exact same things every time, and even more difficult to remember who you told what. But they will.

Whenever you lie you run a terrible risk of losing your own credibility and someone else's trust. There are better ways for you to get your needs met.

YOU'VE GOT THE POWER

If you discover that you are in the habit of telling even little white lies, check with yourself and see if you need some nurturing.

- ☐ Are you hearing some of those messages you learned as a child that you weren't good enough or even worthless?

- ☐ Erase the tape and substitute new and positive statements. Say, "I am likable as I am."

☐ Tell yourself that you are valuable and that you *do* have power in your life.

☐ Say, "People will like the real me when I give them the chance."

WHAT TO DO AND SAY

▶ *You don't feel as successful or respected as you'd like to be, so you "beef up" your achievements.*

Generally, if you're not as successful as you think you could be, find out what in yourself is holding you back. With respect, it may be a reflection of the lack of respect you have for yourself, and you may need to work on that.

▶ *In relationships, you find yourself acting like who you think you "should" be instead of who you really are.*

When you act the way you think you should, instead of the way you are, you're not giving people the chance to know the real you. They may not like the fake person half as much as they could like the genuine one.

Also, you can only keep up the pretense for so long before you start to slip. Other people may then feel betrayed because you weren't being honest with them. Take the risk of being real. If you're not accepted, it's better knowing now rather than wasting your time on someone who's not worth your effort.

▶ *As a manager, you have made certain promises to your employees and now know you will be unable to deliver them. You are stuck.*

As a boss, tell your employees: "I really believed that it was possible to give you what I promised, but I was wrong. Instead of any more promises, let's work toward achieving them in the future. We can brainstorm ideas and discuss ways for us to see them realized."

YOU DON'T OWE ANYONE

You don't owe anyone anything, though there are times when another will tell you that you do. Understand that he is simply trying to take care of himself—and it is *not* in your best interest to respond.

The predicament begins when you are given something that you didn't ask for in the first place, including your life. Parents who place the responsibility on a child for being in existence are simply failing to take responsibility for their own sexual habits. They may be angry at a Higher Power for turning their sexuality into a child. Unable to do anything about confronting the Higher Power, they take their frustration out on the youngster. It's called scapegoating.

There are many variations on the theme of being given what you don't ask for, but the basic pattern is the same. You will also get into trouble when another person did something for you that he or she really didn't *want* to do. You will end up with the bill because there is always a price tag attached to people doing what they *should*. Unwilling to take responsibility for their actions, they tally up what you owe them. Don't pay.

If we cannot say "No," it creates the illusion of "owing" something to the one who asks. The lack of emotional power to set limits causes this problem. This situation may occur because as a child we learned that it was considered impolite or disrespectful to say, "No." For some adults, receiving a "No" creates the feeling of being slighted or even cheated. Human beings need what they need when they need it and either take responsibility to get their needs met, shift that responsibility to someone else, or pay the price. When that price is passed down to you, send the bill back.

YOU'VE GOT THE POWER

Remember, you don't owe anyone anything unless you agreed to a deal. Of course, then you pay what you owe.

☐ When someone makes you feel obligated, check and be sure you agreed to the deal ahead of time. Think back to the beginning of the incident to determine how the situation got into the shape its in. Be willing to talk about what is happening and how you feel. Stick to the main issue at hand rather than getting sucked into the repayment plan that the person has laid out for you.

☐ Be straight with any person you are emotionally involved with, clarifying each of your expectations.

☐ Be willing to stand up for your perceptions and refuse to be blackmailed or made to feel guilty that you are not paying a debt that you didn't choose to incur.

WHAT TO DO AND SAY

▶ *Your parents expect you to visit them annually for the holidays. After all they've done for you, sacrificing for so many years so you could have all the best things money could buy, they believe you owe them.*

When parents lay a guilt trip on their children they often are trying to get some attention. This may take the form of words, "You never visit us anymore," or a sad face. Say, "You're important to me. I care about you." Then set out some definite guidelines for phoning and visiting, such as, "I will not be coming home this holiday, but I will see you in the Spring, and I'll call you next week."

If you are confronted with a serious case of emotional debt, you may actually hear the words, "How ungrateful! And after all your mother and I have done for you." Ignore the hook and instead respond to their present feelings. Say, "I realize you want me to be home for the holidays and that you are disappointed. I will see you as soon as I can." Realize they are only trying to get something they want right now and are dragging in old baggage to try to get it.

▶ *Without being asked, your colleague at work helped you out when you weren't feeling good and then got angry that you didn't return the favor when she decided to call it in.*

When you are given a gift voluntarily (that is, with no stated price tag attached) only to find out later that the giver had a hidden agenda, say, "I am sorry you feel I owe you something, but I didn't realize we cut a deal. Next time please be more clear when you offer me help. If you need help now, I will give it if I can."

▶ *You asked a friend to take care of your kids while you went to the doctor. Later you found out your friend did it at great inconvenience. Ever since then, there has been strain in your relationship.*

When a friend fails to say "No" when you asked for help, and the tension you feel between the two of you makes you feel as if she thinks you owe her something, say as kindly as you can, "I feel tension. Did you help me with the kids when you really needed to say 'No' to my request? If you did, I want you to know that it is okay for you to say 'No' to me any time. I'll still be your friend."

Again, go back to the main issue at hand rather than getting sucked into any repayment plan.

 LIFE REALLY ISN'T FAIR

People need to have some sense of control in their lives. Most of us feel secure when we can predict what is going to happen to us. Fairness gives us the feeling that there is a pattern that we can count on. We want to be able to believe that life is fair.

School age children wail painfully about their experiences not being fair. It is frightening to them that they cannot have control. But the truth is, life is not fair.

If you were highly protected while growing up, then the first assault of unfairness may come as a total surprise. The older the individual at the time of the first experience of unfairness, the worse the letdown. Believing that life is fair for twenty-five years, only to find that no one escapes tough times no matter how hard they work or how good they are, is tougher than learning the lesson at eight or nine.

Yet you can overcome and actually grow from unfair situations. Age often brings this realization. Just know that there is a richness in all kinds of experiences, even those that are unfair.

YOU'VE GOT THE POWER

☐ When someone you know has an unfair occurrence in his life, say, "I'm sorry. If there is anything I can do to help you, let me know. I'll do it."

☐ When you are involved in a situation that is unfair, you will recover most readily if you pay attention to the grief process. Let your feelings out. Talk with someone you trust. Share your anger, but keep the lid on acting your anger out against others or taking it out on yourself by using drugs, alcohol, or in other hurtful means. That will only make you hurt more later. Don't get stuck in feeling sorry for yourself.

☐ Remember that you can overcome unfairness. It is better to let yourself realize that life isn't fair *but* you can right the situation by being realistic. This gives you power to recover.

☐ Don't forget the overview: Even when a lot of bad things happen, you will also have a number of good things happen. Take a long-distance view of the situation and you'll see the ebb and flow of life.

☐ When bad things keep happening, stop and ask, "What can I learn from these situations?" You will often find that there is a hidden message.

☐ Open your mind to a view of yourself making good decisions. Say, "I am able to make good decisions."

☐ Resolve that you won't fight with life anymore. Say, "I work in partnership with life through thick and thin."

WHAT TO DO AND SAY

▶ *You fall in love with a wonderful man only to have your happiness shattered when he marries someone else.*

Let yourself go through the grief process. Call in all your favors and let others help you.

▶ *You give many dedicated years to a company only to be laid off or passed over for promotion.*

You can learn that expectations in others, especially companies, are dangerous if you don't have the power to implement what you want.

It's always an error to have only one plan for happiness, so here's your opportunity to learn flexibility. Be flexible with your planning and come up with a new way to enjoy life.

▶ *You take care of your health, go to church, and do all your work responsibly. Your irreligious, lazy neighbor who eats all the wrong things wins the lottery on the same day that you find out you have a major illness.*

When you live the "right" way, expecting certain outcomes, you need to realize we each have our own challenges to face. It's important we do what we do because we *want* to do it, not just for the outcome. View poor health as a challenge and an opportunity to approach life from a new perspective.